Living in America

TEACHER RESOURCE SERIES

Understanding Key Health Issues

New Readers Press

Developed originally by BOCES Geneseo Migrant Center with funding from a U.S. Education Department Office of Vocational and Adult Education, English Literacy and Civics Education Demonstration Grant

BOCES Geneseo Migrant Center Project Developers:
Curriculum Developers:
  Karen Yamamoto
  Jane Hogan, Ed.D
Contributors:
  Patricia Edwards
  Timothy J. Sparling
Graphic Designer:
  Eva McKendry

Special thanks to
  Robert E. Lynch, Director, BOCES Geneseo Migrant Center

Living in America Teacher's Resource Guide: Understanding Key Health Issues
ISBN 978-1-56420-529-2

Printed in the United States of America
9 8 7 6 5 4 3 2

All proceeds from the sale of New Readers Press materials support literacy programs in the United States and worldwide.

Developmental Editor: Paula Schlusberg
Design and Production Manager: Andrea Woodbury
Illustrations: James Wallace, Linda Tiff
Production Specialist: Jeffrey R. Smith
Cover Design: Kimbrly Koennecke

Contents

Introduction to the *Living in America* Curriculum

Welcome to *Living in America,* a curriculum tailored to the needs, interests, and language proficiency of literacy-level adult English Language Learners (ELLs). Originally developed primarily for migrant farmworkers, the curriculum is now designed to address the needs of any ELL with very limited literacy and oral skills. **Effectiveness, efficiency,** and **relevance** are the hallmarks of the curriculum. *Living in America* provides a framework for successful learning, with concise, easy-to-follow directions and a selection of topics relevant to the situations and tasks that adult ELLs confront. The development of the curriculum was grounded in a series of learner-centered questions:

- What situations create problems for non-English-speaking adults?

- What life skills would make living in the U.S. easier for non-English-speaking adults?

- What vocabulary and conversation patterns would help facilitate daily communication?

- What civics information regarding legal issues would be pertinent to adult ELLs?

- What knowledge of rights and responsibilities would support community membership?

The design, materials, and strategies selected for the curriculum were guided by a set of instructor-centered questions:

- What lesson design and accompanying materials would best support instructors using the curriculum?

- What teaching strategies would be applicable to a variety of learners and suitable for the variety of instructional settings where those learners are taught?

The resulting curriculum, *Living in America,* provides literacy learners with functional, everyday language that is essential for successfully navigating a new community. Civics-based lessons paired with life-skill lessons help learners understand basic principles, customs, behaviors, and laws in the U.S. The combination of these lessons gives adult learners a voice and access to their rights and responsibilities as contributing community members.

The term "social civics" can be used for norms of expected behavior in situations where a behavior is inappropriate but not illegal. Behaviors and situations stressed in the curriculum are those which may be different from the norms and values in adult learners' native countries. Carefully selected vocabulary, statements, questions, and related dialogues develop learners' situational language skills, while the civics content fosters understanding and behaviors leading to improved community involvement and acceptance.

The most important force in motivating learners is the instructor's enthusiasm and investment in the curriculum. In *Living in America*, the instructor is the educational decision-maker. Decisions to modify, to reinforce, or to provide more practice are left for the instructor to make.

Approach to Language Learning

The *Living in America* curriculum incorporates an eclectic approach:

- **Communicative Language Instruction** emphasizes the language needed to communicate effectively

- **Total Physical Response** uses nonverbal means of communicating

- **Audio-lingual Instruction** provides the foundation for instructor-directed strategies to teach needed vocabulary and simple sentence patterns within exercises and dialogues

The curriculum focuses on oral competency and comprehension skills, so that learners are able to make their needs known and to understand the information given in response to their questions. Grammar is modeled in the curriculum but not explicitly explained. The curriculum takes the position that if a beginning speaker is understood, sentence form is not as important as the meaning conveyed. Integrating other ESL materials with the *Living in America* curriculum is encouraged and expected, especially to build prerequisite knowledge, including everyday vocabulary as well as letters, colors, dates, numbers, and times.

The Curriculum

Living in America consists of six teacher's resource guides (TRGs). Each TRG presents four to six units on thematically grouped topics. A list of the TRGs and the units in each is found at the end of this Introduction (p. 14). A unit contains two lessons, each designed to be approximately 120 to 180 minutes in length. The four to six instructional hours can be divided flexibly to meet learners' needs and the demands of the instructional setting.

Research-Based Strategies

- Model everything first
- Use gestures and body language
- Use realia or authentic materials
- Proceed in a clear instructional sequence: Oral Language → Reading → Writing
- Use a limited number of vocabulary words
- Use and practice vocabulary throughout the lesson
- Proceed from Instructor Model → Group Practice → Individual Practice
- Build on prior knowledge
- Give genuine, positive feedback
- Promote a learning environment that is cooperative, not competitive
- Use constant and consistent repetition and review
- Maintain high, yet reasonable expectations
- Focus on oral understanding and production of English

Curriculum Features

The curriculum embodies the following:

- **Life skills are paired with civics skills** for successful adjustment to living in and navigating the communities of the U.S.

- **Specific topics are nonsequential,** so that learners' needs and interests can guide topic selection

- **Lessons are adaptable** to any formal or informal learning environment and may be used with groups of various sizes

- **Listening and speaking are emphasized** to meet the needs of beginning learners, who may not be literate in their native languages

- **Research-based teaching strategies are woven** into all lesson activities and learner exercises (see sidebar)

- **A variety of learning styles is supported,** through cues supporting the needs of both visual and auditory learners, and through application activities supporting kinesthetic (hands-on) learners

- **Graphics, vocabulary cards, interactive activities, and activity sheets are included** to facilitate lesson planning and teaching

- **A civics introduction gives background information** about the legal principle supporting each civics lesson

Lesson Features

The lessons are designed to set learners up for success. Because of this, it is desirable to conduct lessons in English. Gestures, mime, drawings, and realia can be used to clarify and enhance understanding and learning. It is best to limit word-for-word translation from the learners' first language. Abstract concepts are an exception, since they are often difficult to comprehend without the support of a first language.

Each lesson includes:

- **Core vocabulary,** illustrated whenever possible and presented on cards
- **Scripted models** of dialogue patterns
- **Suggestions for support gestures and teacher remarks** for eliciting responses and giving praise
- **Model scripts** of oral lesson interactions, where I = Instructor, G = Group, and L = Learner

- **A patterned progression of activities** and repeated activity types to provide consistency for the learners and ease of delivery for the instructor

Lesson Components

Lesson A: Life Skill

- the central theme picture
- four oral language activities
- comprehension checks
- a reading activity
- a writing activity

Lesson B: Civic Responsibility

- a civics introduction
- a storyboard (as appropriate)
- four oral language activities
- comprehension checks
- a reading activity
- a writing activity

Unit Review Activity

Oral Language Activities: Both life-skill and civic-responsibility lessons contain four oral language activities. These begin with interactive vocabulary development, including opportunities for multiple repetition of each target word or phrase. Vocabulary is introduced in a consistent manner for each oral language activity.

Practice Exercises: In each oral language activity, there are practice exercises that incorporate review, enrichment, and application. These practice exercises either allow for cooperative learning or may involve concept development. All exercises model an example of teacher-student interaction and provide step-by-step instructions for easy reference.

Dialogues: Dialogues relate to the theme picture, storyboard, or lesson content. They model a simple conversation appropriate to the context of that lesson. Vocabulary and sentence patterns taught in the lesson are used in the dialogue, providing an opportunity for learners to practice short, focused conversations.

Comprehension Checks: The comprehension check at the end of an activity is a simple and efficient means of assessing whether the material and concepts have been learned. The checks are meant to be done quickly in order to establish whether there is a need for additional practice or whether the group should move forward in the lesson.

Skill Enhancements: Each lesson includes optional reading and writing activities. In reading activities, learners practice recognizing written forms of words or phrases within the context of the lesson. Whenever appropriate, writing activities provide an authentic task, so learners can practice writing something they can use later, like a list of emergency telephone numbers or a repair checklist.

Lesson Support Materials

Each *Living in America* TRG includes photocopy masters (PCMs) of graphics, vocabulary cards, interactive activities, and activity sheets needed to plan and teach lessons. A generic PCM with **OK/Not OK** cards is at the end of the book. In the units, each lesson includes a list of the PCMs needed for that lesson. These unit-specific PCMs follow the lesson notes for each unit. Some of the PCMs will be used multiple times in the lessons, and multiple sets of other PCMs will be needed for some activities. Therefore, copying or pasting them onto card stock or other heavy paper is advisable.

The lessons also include suggestions for realia or authentic materials to use in explaining or enhancing lesson content and activities. These suggestions include real or instructor-made documents, visuals from newspapers or magazines, and real objects.

Central Theme Picture and Storyboard: In each unit, the PCMs begin with a theme picture, introduced in Lesson A: Life Skill. This theme picture provides the context for the lesson. It can also be used to assess prior knowledge or provide a link to the learners' backgrounds. Lesson B: Civic Responsibility begins, when appropriate, with a storyboard of four frames, used primarily to demonstrate the civics concept under discussion. This storyboard is also often woven into the lesson itself.

Vocabulary Cards: In all lessons, large vocabulary cards include a graphic representation, or picture cue, and a target word or phrase to be presented simultaneously. Some lessons also include a set of small picture cards with just the graphic representation and a set of small word cards. The word is first taught orally. The print form becomes "environmental print" while the instructor refers to the graphic in the lessons. Learners may use the picture cues in all activities to provide support. Later in the lesson, the print forms of the words or phrases are the focus of the optional reading and writing activities.

Activity Sheets: Reproducible activity sheets are provided for selected activities and may be completed as a group or by individual learners. Most activity sheets are presented orally. They stress graphic representations rather than written words, to help learners succeed regardless of their reading level or ability. Teachers may want to create enlarged versions of activity sheets for ease in modeling or reviewing activities.

Unit Review Activities for Assessment: Each unit includes a review activity that can be used to assess and provide a written record of learner progress. These unit reviews mirror the kinds of exercises learners have done throughout the lessons. They combine the life skill and the civic responsibility being taught. The term *Review* is used rather than *Assessment* to minimize learners' test anxiety.

Selected Teaching Techniques

The *Living in America* curriculum uses language teaching techniques that research has shown to be appropriate for adult learners and effective with learners with limited or no prior exposure to English. The techniques suggested can be used with individuals or with groups of various sizes. They can also be modified for learners with more advanced abilities. Models and clear steps are provided within each activity to provide direction for the instructor.

Assessment of Prior Knowledge: Prior knowledge is assessed at the beginning of each lesson using the theme picture or the storyboard. The instructor points to elements of the picture that represent key themes in the lesson and gives learners time to make associations, name or point out objects, and preview new words.

Introduction of Target Vocabulary: Target, or core, vocabulary is practiced in each oral language activity. New words or terms are learned in the context of the theme picture or storyboard. Graphic representations of words, available on the vocabulary cards, are also effective tools for introducing vocabulary. Mime and/or gestures are used to model actions, elicit responses, or explain complex concepts when new vocabulary is difficult to represent graphically.

Modeling: Instructors are provided with suggestions and examples of how to model vocabulary within the context of each lesson. Modeling accurate pronunciation and usage is important for beginning ELLs.

Repetition: Repetition is the key to helping language learners develop quick, natural responses. Activity and exercise guidelines suggest repeating every word, phrase, and sentence pattern three times, or more if necessary. Learners repeat target vocabulary as a group before individuals are asked to produce the vocabulary on their own.

Dialogues: Mini-dialogues and role plays of two to four sentences are introduced within activities. Longer dialogues are often introduced to present conversation patterns or to develop understanding of a civics concept.

Gestures: Use gestures to indicate when the learners should listen, respond, stop, wait, or take turns. Use gestures consistently to provide nonverbal cues during lessons.

Backward Buildup: This technique is employed by breaking a target sentence into parts and starting with repetition of the last phrase. For example: *I am going / to the store / to buy milk.* Teach *to buy milk* first. When the learner can say *to buy milk,* teach *to the store.* Combine the two. Then teach *I am going.* Finally, model the entire sentence and have the learners repeat it as one unit.

Substitution: Teach a target pattern, and then replace a word or phrase with another that completes the sentence. For example: *He is her husband.* After the learner can say this sentence, replace the initial target, *husband,* with *brother.* For example:

> **I:** "He is her husband."
> **I:** "Brother."
> **L:** "He is her brother."

Error Correction: Correct only when a learner's answer does not convey the correct meaning. State the correct response and ask learners to restate the correct answer. For example, the learner is asked to indicate that the windshield is broken, but responds with a reference to the tire.

> **I:** "What is broken?" (Point to windshield.)
> **L:** "The tire is broken."
> **I:** "Windshield. The windshield is broken." (Motion for the learner to repeat.)
> **L:** "The windshield is broken."

Modified Input: When the learner does not have the language facility to reproduce a complete sentence, speech can be modified by dropping articles, verbs, and inflectional endings. For example: *Windshield broken* or *Not OK.* With simplified grammar, the meaning is clearer to the learner. A learner response in modified speech or using a one-word answer would not be corrected, as long as the correct meaning is conveyed.

Reinforcement: Give immediate and genuine reinforcement when a learner gives a correct answer. Use words like *good, good work, OK, yes, right,* and *terrific.* Restatement of a correct answer is also a form of positive reinforcement.

Preparation for Using *Living in America*

Prior to implementing the *Living in America* curriculum, familiarize yourself with the lesson content. Preview each lesson, to make notes for quick reference and to gather or duplicate graphics, activity sheets, and additional materials needed for the lesson.

Many resources are available to instructors and learners in the field of ESL. Search local libraries or look online for materials that are appropriate for the level of ELLs being served and that contribute to professional development. A list of useful search topics is provided in the sidebar.

Useful Search Topics

- Adult Learners
- Civics Education
- EL-Civics
- English Language Learner (ELL)
- English as a Second Language (ESL)
- English for Speakers of Other Languages (ESOL)
- Immigrant Education
- Literacy
- Migrant Education
- ProLiteracy Worldwide
- Refugee Education
- Teaching English to Speakers of Other Languages (TESOL)

The *Living in America* Curriculum

Getting Along with Others
Introducing Yourself
Marking Your Calendar
Understanding Families
Protecting Yourself and Others
Understanding Manners in the U.S.

Using Official Documents
Using Money
Saving Necessary Documents
Finding Work
Preparing for Tax Time

Fitting into Your Community
Going to the Store
Recycling
Navigating the Community
Using the Phone
Paying for Phone Calls
Riding a Bicycle

Understanding Key Health Issues
Using Doctor and Hospital Services
Handling Dangerous Chemicals
Medicine and Controlled Substances
Having Safe Relationships

Operating a Motor Vehicle
Getting Ready to Drive
Driving
Owning a Car
Keeping Your Car Running
Maintaining Your Car
Navigating the Roads

Knowing Your Rights and Responsibilities
Getting a Lawyer
Communicating with Neighbors and the Police
Understanding Community Responsibilities
Understanding a Lease
Maintaining Housing

Unit 1

Using Doctor and Hospital Services

Lesson A - Life Skill

Body Parts & Medical Conditions

VOCABULARY

NOUNS

Arm	Hand
Back	Head
Chest	Leg
Ear	Stomach
Eye	Throat
Foot	

POSSESSIVE PRONOUN

My

ADJECTIVES

Broken

Burned

Cut

VERB

Hurts

QUESTION/ANSWERS

What's wrong?

My head hurts.

My leg is broken.

Objectives

- To enable learners to identify parts of the body
- To enable learners to say what is wrong in the event of an illness

Materials Included

- Central theme picture
- Large reproducible vocabulary cards
- Body Part Labeling activity sheet
- Noun spinner, Adjectives and Verb spinner
- Word Search activity sheet
- Label the Parts of the Body activity sheet
- **Yes/No** cards

Materials Needed

- Additional instructor copy (enlarged) of the activity sheets
- Pictures of matches and a knife (or real items)
- Picture of a person bleeding from a cut
- Two paper fasteners

Central Theme Picture

MATERIALS

Theme picture

Introduce the Theme Picture

1. Show learners the theme picture and ask for a response.
2. Encourage learners to say anything about the picture that they can.

> **I:** "What's happening in this picture?" (Point out key things about the picture to elicit a response.)

Possible Responses

Broken

Cut

Doctor

Form

Hospital

Man

Nurse

Office

Woman

Oral Language Activity 1

MATERIALS

Large noun cards

Body Part Labeling activity sheet (one enlarged)

Yes/No cards (one set per learner)

Introduce the Target Nouns

1. Hold up each vocabulary card and motion for learners to repeat each term.

> **I:** "Arm." (Hold up the **arm** card. Motion for the learners to repeat the word.)
> **G:** "Arm."
> **I:** "Good. Arm." (Motion for learners to repeat the word.)
> **G:** "Arm."
> **I:** "Very good. What's this?" (Point to your own arm. Hold up the **arm** card. Motion for a response.)
> **G:** "Arm."

2. Introduce other parts of the body following the steps above.
3. Have all learners repeat each word three times.
4. Shuffle the cards after they have been introduced. Show them at random to the learners and elicit responses for more verbal practice.
5. Continue on to the activity when learners can identify each vocabulary term without assistance.

Body Part Labeling Activity

1. Hold up each target noun card and have the group say each word to review the vocabulary for parts of the body.

2. Point to appropriate parts of your own body to reinforce the new vocabulary. Encourage the group to point to the parts of their own body and repeat each term.
3. Shuffle all of the noun cards together.
4. Post an enlarged copy of the Body Part Labeling activity sheet in the front of the room or another visible location.
5. Distribute the set of noun cards to learners by placing each card facedown on the table or other surface in front of a learner. If there are more learners than cards, repeat the activity until all learners have had at least one turn with a card.
6. Have each learner take a turn picking up their card and identifying the vocabulary term.
7. Ask each learner to approach the enlarged Body Part Labeling activity sheet and place the card in the correct place or draw an arrow as appropriate.
8. Gesture for the group to repeat each word after the body is labeled.

Comprehension Check

1. Distribute a set of **Yes/No** cards to each learner.
2. Place the body outline at the front of the room.
3. Hold up each noun card and point to that part of the body on the activity sheet.
4. Identify the part correctly and incorrectly at random.
5. Have the learners hold up a **Yes** card when the term is identified correctly and a **No** card when the term is identified incorrectly.

> **I:** "Arm." (Hold up the **arm** card. Point to the arm on the activity sheet.)
>
> **I:** "Arm." (Hold up the **arm** card. Hold up the **Yes** card.)
>
> **I:** "Yes." (Motion for the group to repeat.)
>
> **G:** "Yes." (Learners should hold up the **Yes** card.)
>
> **I:** "Chest." (Hold up the **leg** card. Motion for a response.)
>
> **G:** "No." (Learners should hold up the **No** card.)

Oral Language Activity 2

MATERIALS

Large adjective cards (multiple copies)

Large verb card (multiple copies)

Large noun cards

Pictures of matches, a knife, and a person bleeding from a cut

Theme picture

Noun spinner, Adjectives and Verb spinner

Introduce the Adjectives and Verb

1. Introduce the verb **hurts** by miming physical pain.

> **I:** "Hurts." (Hold up the **hurts** card. Show **hurts** by miming a headache or stomachache or hitting a finger with a hammer. Motion for the learners to repeat.)
>
> **G:** "Hurts."
>
> **I:** "Good. Hurts." (Motion for learners to repeat together.)
>
> **G:** "Hurts."
>
> **I:** "Very good. What's wrong?" (Show **hurts** by miming a headache, backache, or stomachache. Motion for a response.)
>
> **G:** "Hurts."

2. Introduce **broken, burned,** and **cut** using the method above.

3. Reinforce the adjective **cut** through mime and/or pictures. Use the picture of the knife to reinforce the meaning. Show the picture of matches to reinforce **burned.**

4. Have learners repeat each term three times.

5. Shuffle the cards after they have been introduced. Show them at random to the learners and elicit responses for more verbal practice.

6. Post the noun, adjective, and verb cards on the board, on chart paper, or in another visible location.

7. Make columns with the noun, adjective, and verb cards by placing the nouns in a column on the left and the adjectives and verb (**cut, burned, broken,** and **hurts**) in a column on the right.

8. Point to each of the noun cards and elicit responses.

> **I:** "What's this?" (Point to the **leg** card. Motion for a response.)
>
> **G:** "Leg."
>
> **I:** "Good. Leg." (Point to the **leg** card.)

9. Combine the noun card with an adjective or verb card by first having learners identify an appropriate adjective or verb to go with the noun.

> **I:** "What's this?" (Hold up the **broken** card. Motion for a response.)
>
> **G:** "Broken."
>
> **I:** "Good. Broken."

Lesson A *Life Skill* **19**

10. Reposition the **broken** card in the adjective/verb column to the right of the **leg** card to make a pair.

> **I:** "Leg is broken." (Point to the **broken** card and then to the **leg** card. Motion for the group to repeat the phrase.)
>
> **G:** "Leg is broken."
>
> **I:** "Leg is broken." (Point to the **broken** card and then to the **leg** card and motion for the group to repeat.)
>
> **G:** "Leg is broken."

11. Continue to pair nouns with adjectives or the verb to make phrases and have the group repeat each phrase at least three times.

Sample Pairs

Nouns	Adjectives/Verb
hand, arm, foot, leg	broken
ear, hand, foot, arm, leg	cut
hand, arm, foot, leg	burned
stomach, chest, head, ear, back, throat, eye	hurts

NOTE

Prepare spinners by attaching the arrows to the circles of pictures with a two-pronged paper fastener.

Have learners spin again if the combination of terms does not make sense. For example, if a learner spins *eye* and *broken*, the learner should spin again for a different condition.

Spin Activity

1. Show the group the noun spinner and the adjectives and verb spinner.
2. Place the spinners in the center of the group.
3. Have one learner spin both spinners and identify the phrase that results, as in the example below.

> **I:** "What's this?" (Point to the picture of the **arm** on the noun spinner and the picture of **cut** on the adjectives and verb spinner. Motion for a response.)
>
> **L:** "Arm is cut."

4. Continue having each learner take a turn to spin both spinners and identify the phrases correctly.
5. Use the suggested pairs in step 11 above as a guide to acceptable responses.

Comprehension Check

1. Distribute a set of **Yes/No** cards to each learner.
2. Hold up two vocabulary cards, one noun and one adjective or verb. Identify the phrase made by the cards either correctly or incorrectly, at random.
3. Have the group respond to each correctly identified phrase by saying Yes and holding up the **Yes** card and to each incorrectly identified phrase by saying No and holding up the **No** card.

> **I:** "Arm is cut." (Hold up the **arm** and **cut** cards. Motion for a response from the group.)
>
> **I:** "Arm is cut. Yes." (Hold up the **Yes** card. Motion for the group to respond.)
>
> **G:** "Yes." (Learners should hold up the **Yes** card.)
>
> **I:** "Leg is broken." (Hold up the **eye** and **cut** cards. Motion for the group to respond.)
>
> **G:** "No." (Learners should hold up the **No** card.)

4. Continue with other combinations to check the group's understanding of the vocabulary.

Oral Language Activity 3

MATERIALS

Large vocabulary cards

Introduce the Possessive Pronoun

1. Use the noun cards with the pronoun **my** to help learners understand the concept of possession.

> **I:** "Hand. My hand." (Hold up the **hand** card. Point to yourself. Hold up your own hand. Motion for the learners to repeat.)
>
> **G:** "My hand." (Learners should hold up their hands.)
>
> **I:** "Good. My." (Point to yourself. Motion for learners to repeat together.)
>
> **G:** "My." (Learners should point to themselves.)
>
> **I:** "Very good. My." (Point to yourself. Motion for the learners to repeat.)
>
> **G:** "My." (Learners should point to themselves.)

2. Have learners identify various parts of the body (**arm, back, chest, ear, eye, foot, hand, head, leg, stomach,** and **throat**) using **my.**
3. Model the phrase and point to your own body part to clarify for learners as necessary.

Make a Sentence Activity

1. Use **my** with parts of the body to build sentences.

> **I:** "What's this?" (Hold up the **foot** card. Motion for a response.)
>
> **G:** "Foot."
>
> **I:** "My foot." (Hold up the **foot** card. Point to your own foot. Motion for the learners to repeat.)
>
> **G:** "My foot." (Learners should point to their feet.)
>
> **I:** "Good. My foot." (Hold up the **foot** card. Point to your own foot. Motion for the learners to repeat.)
>
> **G:** "My foot." (Learners should point to their feet.)
>
> **I:** "What's this?" (Hold up the **cut** card. Motion for a response.)
>
> **G:** "Cut."
>
> **I:** "Yes. My foot is cut." (Hold up the **foot** and **cut** cards. Motion for learners to repeat.)
>
> **G:** "My foot is cut."

2. Use combinations of vocabulary cards from Oral Language Activity 2 to help learners build other sentences.
3. Place the noun cards and the adjective and verb cards facedown in two separate piles on the table or other flat surface in the center of the group.
4. Draw a card from each pile and make a sentence using **my,** as in the example below.

> **I:** "My head hurts." (Hold up the **head** and **hurts** cards. Motion for learners to repeat.)
>
> **G:** "My head hurts."

5. Have learners take turns drawing cards from each pile and making sentences using the cards drawn.
6. Have the learners read their sentences aloud. Then have learners return the cards to the bottom of the appropriate piles.
7. Reshuffle the cards and repeat the activity more than one time for more verbal practice.

Comprehension Check

1. Hold up two sets of paired vocabulary cards (a noun with an adjective or verb).
2. Say a sentence using the words from one set. Have learners point to the correct pair and repeat the whole sentence.

Examples

eye/hurts	foot/broken

> **I:** "My foot is broken." (Motion for the group to point to the corresponding pair. Ask the learners to repeat the sentence.)
>
> **G:** "My foot is broken." (Learners should point to the **foot** and **broken** cards.)

3. Continue with various sets of vocabulary pairs to check the group's understanding.

Oral Language Activity 4

MATERIALS

Large vocabulary cards

Yes/No cards (one set for each learner)

Introduce the Dialogue

1. Write the sample dialogue (see example below) on the board or other available surface. Read it for the group, pointing to each word.
2. Use the large vocabulary cards to prompt the responses and clarify the meaning. Mime or use pictures to demonstrate the meaning.

> **Speaker 1:** "What's wrong?" (Hold up the **chest** card. Mime having a pain in your chest to illustrate **hurts.** Motion for the group to respond.)
>
> **Speaker 2:** "My chest hurts."
>
> **Speaker 1:** "What's wrong?" (Hold up the **leg** and **broken** cards. Motion for a response.)
>
> **Speaker 2:** "My leg is broken."
>
> **Speaker 1:** "What's wrong?" (Hold up the **hand** and **cut** cards. Motion for a response.)
>
> **Speaker 2:** "My hand is cut."
>
> **Speaker 1:** "What's wrong?" (Hold up the **arm** and **burned** cards. Motion for a response.)
>
> **Speaker 2:** "My arm is burned."

NOTE

Pointing to each word while reading is important to do even if the learners are non-readers or nonliterate.

3. Point to each word whenever the dialogue is repeated in this activity.
4. Intoduce the dialogue, with the instructor as Speaker 1 and have the group respond as Speaker 2. Ask the question, prompt learners by holding up the appropriate noun and adjective or verb cards, and motion for a response.
5. Repeat the dialogue, substituting other nouns that go with the adjectives and verb in the responses.

Dialogue Activity

1. Write the model dialogue (see example below) on the board or other available surface. Read it for the group, pointing to each word.

> **I:** "What's wrong?" (Hold up the **chest** card. Mime having a pain in your chest to illustrate **hurts.** Motion for the group to respond.)
>
> **G:** "My chest hurts."
>
> **I:** "What's wrong?" (Hold up the **leg** and **broken** cards. Motion for a response.)
>
> **G:** "My leg is broken."
>
> **I:** "What's wrong?" (Hold up the **hand** and **cut** cards. Motion for a response.)
>
> **G:** "My hand is cut."
>
> **I:** "What's wrong?" (Hold up the **arm** and **burned** cards. Motion for a response.)
>
> **G:** "My arm is burned."

2. Point to each word whenever the dialogue is repeated in this activity.
3. Introduce the dialogue and have the group respond to your prompts.
4. Perform the dialogue as a group three times using the vocabulary cards as necessary to prompt the responses.
5. Vary the combinations of cards to prompt different responses.
6. Prompt learners to start the dialogue. Put a question mark on the board or on chart paper. Model the question and have learners repeat.

> **I:** "What's wrong?" (Point to the question mark. Motion for learners to repeat.)
>
> **G:** "What's wrong?"
>
> **I:** "What's wrong?" (Point to the question mark. Motion for learners to repeat.)
>
> **G:** "What's wrong?"

7. Point to the question mark and motion for learners to ask the question. Respond to their question, holding up the cards that correspond to the response.

> **G:** "What's wrong?"
>
> **I:** "My arm is broken." (Hold up the **arm** and **broken** cards.)

8. Divide learners into two groups. Prompt one group to ask the question, by pointing to the question mark. Prompt the other group to respond while holding up a pair of vocabulary cards.

9. After several repetitions of the dialogue, have the groups reverse roles.

Comprehension Check

1. Distribute a set of **Yes/No** cards to each learner.
2. Hold up two vocabulary cards, one noun and one adjective or verb, and say a complete sentence.
3. Say correct and incorrect sentences (corresponding to the cards or not corresponding) at random.
4. Have the group identify the correct sentences by holding up the **Yes** card and the incorrect sentences by holding up the **No** card.
5. Model and prompt responses before asking learners to respond independently.

> **I:** "My leg is broken." (Hold up the **leg** and **broken** cards.)
>
> **I:** "My leg is broken. Yes." (Hold up the **Yes** card. Nod head to indicate Yes. Motion for the group to respond.)
>
> **G:** "Yes." (Learners should hold up the **Yes** card.)
>
> **I:** "My ear hurts." (Hold up the **leg** and **broken** cards. Shake head to indicate No. Motion for the group to respond.)
>
> **G:** "No." (Learners should hold up the **No** card.)

Reading Activity

MATERIALS

Large vocabulary cards

Word Search activity sheet (one enlarged and one per learner)

Review

1. Shuffle the large vocabulary cards.
2. Show each card to the group while pronouncing each word slowly and clearly.
3. Run a finger under each word to help learners begin to recognize the words apart from the pictures.
4. Have the learners repeat the words at least three times.

> **I:** "Arm." (Point to the word.)
>
> **G:** "Arm."
>
> **I:** "Arm." (Underline the word with a finger. Motion for the group to repeat the word.)
>
> **G:** "Arm."

NOTE

Separating words from pictures should be done gradually and after plenty of practice.

5. Continue to review with the cards, using the pattern above.
6. Fold cards in half to show only the words, to help learners become less dependent on the pictures.

7. Move from group to individual practice as learners become more comfortable reading the words without the assistance of the pictures.

Word Search Activity

1. Pass out a Word Search activity sheet to each learner.
2. Put the enlarged copy of the activity sheet in the front of the room or in another visible location.
3. Point to each picture at the top of the enlarged activity sheet and ask learners to identify the picture verbally. Run a finger under the word next to the picture and motion for learners to read the word.
4. Using the enlarged activity sheet, show the learners how to use the pictures and words listed at the top to locate words in the word search grid.
5. Choose a word from the list to locate in the word search grid.
6. Read the word for the learners and point to the picture that represents it.
7. Demonstrate how to look in the word search grid for the word written next to the picture.
8. Model finding the word, pointing to each letter in the word. Then demonstrate on the enlarged sheet how to circle the word that is found.
9. Have the learners say each word from the list before they begin their search. Have them complete their own Word Search activity sheets.
10. Assist learners as necessary.
11. When learners have completed their activity sheets, have volunteers come up and circle the rest of the words on the enlarged activity sheet.
12. Check learners' reading by pointing to a circled word on the enlarged activity sheet and having learners read the word.

Writing Activity

MATERIALS

Large vocabulary cards

Body Part Labeling activity sheet (enlarged)

Label the Parts of the Body activity sheet (one enlarged and one for each learner)

Review

1. Shuffle the large vocabulary cards.
2. Show each card to the group while pronouncing each word slowly and clearly.
3. Run a finger under each word to help learners begin to recognize the words apart from the pictures.
4. Have the learners repeat the words at least three times.

> **I:** "Chest." (Point to the word.)
>
> **G:** "Chest."
>
> **I:** "Chest." (Underline the word with a finger. Motion for the group to repeat the word.)
>
> **G:** "Chest."

NOTE

Separating words from pictures should be done gradually and after plenty of practice.

5. Continue to review with the cards, using the pattern above.
6. Fold cards in half to show only the words, to help learners become less dependent on the pictures.
7. Move from group to individual practice as learners become more comfortable reading the words without the assistance of the pictures.

Label the Parts of the Body Activity

1. Display the vocabulary cards in the front of the room or in another visible location for learners to use as a reference.
2. Distribute the Label the Parts of the Body activity sheet to each learner.
3. Put an enlarged copy of the activity sheet in the front of the room or in another visible location.
4. On the enlarged activity sheet, point to one part of the body at a time and have the group identify each.
5. Point to the lines next to each part of the body. Show the group that each vocabulary word should be written on the line next to the corresponding body part.
6. If needed, display the enlarged labeled outline of the body from Oral Language Activity 1 to model for learners how to write the names of the parts of the body on the lines.
7. Assist learners as necessary.

Lesson B - Civic Responsibility

Emergency Room

VOCABULARY

NOUNS
Cough

Doctor

ER (Emergency Room)

Fever

Hospital

Interpreter

QUESTION

Where do you go?

Objective

To enable learners to determine what medical problems are serious enough to require treatment in the hospital emergency room and which can be treated in the doctor's office

Adapting Lesson Activities

In these lesson activities, learners are asked to decide what medical conditions call for seeing a doctor and what conditions call for a visit to a hospital emergency room. Items are sorted into "doctor" or "hospital ER" on the basis of what is generally or most likely going to be appropriate. For the sake of consistency and simplicity, learners can work with the choices presented here. If at all possible, however, help learners understand that in some cases, the conditions can be very mild and treated even without a doctor's attention (e.g., a simple cut or relatively mild backache), while in other cases, even broken bones, the conditions can be treated in a doctor's office if they do not seem life-threatening and if they can be controlled easily. Learners need to understand that going to the hospital emergency room should be reserved for extreme instances of health problems or for situations in which a person cannot get to a doctor but does need immediate attention. For example, a cut hand might require a small bandage from a first aid kit, or it might involve bleeding that cannot be controlled, requiring immediate treatment in an ER.

Materials Included

- Large reproducible vocabulary cards
- Sorting activity sheet
- Circle the Correct Word activity sheet
- Sort and Write activity sheet
- **OK/Not OK** cards (page 208)

Materials Needed

- Additional instructor copy (enlarged) of the activity sheets
- A digital thermometer
- Yarn
- Number cards (100-103)

Civics Introduction

Emergency Room

In the U.S., an individual who is sick or injured can go for treatment to a doctor or the hospital emergency room, depending on the severity of the condition. Sudden illness, routine health problems, or minor injuries can be treated in a doctor's office. If an immediate appointment is needed, offices can generally accommodate an unscheduled visit with limited prior notice. Extreme injuries and severe illnesses should be treated in a hospital emergency room. Hospitals have more equipment and personnel to treat severe emergency health situations than doctors' offices.

Health care systems have a code of patient rights in place to protect the patient and maintain quality of services. For a non-English-speaking patient, interpreter services must be provided as part of the patient's rights. Also, emergency care must be administered regardless of a patient's income and/or lack of insurance.

This topic is important to newly arrived, non-English-speaking adults because they may be accustomed to different systems of health care and to different criteria for deciding where to go for treatment, whether for minor or severe health problems. They need to understand how to determine whether a health problem is so severe that it requires immediate treatment in an emergency room. Additionally, it is important for non-English-speaking adults to know that in most states, interpretation services are available, even required, when health care is being provided.

It is important for new arrivals to become familiar with their state's health care rights and programs. Hospitals and service agencies can provide assistance and guidance in helping these individuals understand their rights to health care. Understanding those rights can be particularly important for immigrants with irregular residency status.

Because emergency rooms are often misused as a source of treatment for even relatively minor medical problems or to manage chronic health problems, people need to understand where to go for help. They should have a clear understanding of whether they should visit (or take their children to) the doctor's office or the emergency room when needing treatment for an injury or illness. If they do not have access to or a relationship with a regular doctor, they need to be made aware of alternative medical facilities, such as clinics run by community health services, so that they can avoid relying inappropriately on hospital emergency rooms.

Oral Language Activity 1

MATERIALS

Large noun cards (from Lessons A & B, two sets)

Digital thermometer

Yes/No cards (one set for each learner)

NOTE

Teach **fever** using the **thermometer** card and a real thermometer or illustration. Show that normal body temperature is 98.6 degrees Fahrenheit, a mild fever is between 100 and 102 degrees Fahrenheit, and a severe fever is 103 or more degrees Fahrenheit.

Teach learners to say **ER** but recognize that it means **Emergency Room,** so that they can understand signs at hospitals. Where appropriate, have them say the terms together **(hospital ER).**

Hospitals and doctors' offices are required to provide interpreters when needed. The term **interpreter** is introduced in this lesson so that newly arrived, non-English speaking adults are aware that an interpreter should be provided when necessary and that if an interpreter is not provided, they should ask for one.

Introduce the Target Nouns

1. Show each large noun card (**cough, doctor, ER, fever,** and **hospital**) to the group while pronouncing each word slowly and clearly.

> **I:** "Cough." (Hold up the **cough** card and motion for the group to repeat.)
> **G:** "Cough."
> **I:** "Cough." (Hold up the **cough** card and motion for the group to repeat.)
> **G:** "Cough."
> **I:** "Cough." (Hold up the **cough** card and motion for the group to repeat.)
> **G:** "Cough."

2. Teach **interpreter** using simple pairs of words in English and other languages, if possible. Try to use the native language(s) of your learners.

> **I:** "Interpreter." (Hold up the **doctor** card, point to it, and say a simple word or phrase in English. Post the card on the board or on chart paper, and write the English word or phrase in a speech bubble above the **doctor** card. Say **interpreter,** point to yourself, and say the same thing in a second language, or if possible, in more than one language. Motion for the group to repeat.)
> **I:** "Interpreter." (Point to the doctor's words in English, point to yourself, and say the words in the second language. Repeat **interpreter** and motion for learners to repeat.)
> **G:** "Interpreter."

3. Use mime, gestures, or realia to support learners' understanding of the vocabulary.
4. Say each word and have the group repeat each one three times.
5. Repeat any words more than three times if necessary, with the group, with pairs, or individually.

NOTE

Photocopying each set of noun cards on a different color of paper will facilitate the matching of pairs for this activity. This can be a noncompetitive group activity or learners can remove the cards when they make a match. The learner with the most matched pairs wins.

Concentration

1. Shuffle two sets of large noun cards (from Lessons A and B) together.
2. Spread cards out on the table or other visible surface facedown so that they are not overlapping.
3. Model the activity by turning over two cards. Show one failure and one success.
4. Identify or have the learners identify the cards.
5. Model getting a matched pair to show how a player with a matched pair keeps the cards and is allowed an extra turn.
6. Model getting cards that do not match to show how those cards must be put back facedown on the table.
7. Motion for learners to begin the activity by choosing the first person to start.
8. Have each learner choose two cards and identify both of them.
9. Motion for the learners to hold up their pairs or cards to show the group as they identify them.
10. When the activity is finished, have learners say which pairs they collected.
11. Count each learner's pairs of cards, and encourage the group to count along.
12. Repeat any of the words that learners have trouble remembering for more verbal practice.
13. Assist learners as needed.

NOTE

For this activity, learners will need to understand and be able to distinguish between the words **Yes** and **No.**

Comprehension Check

1. Distribute a set of **Yes/No** cards to each learner.
2. Collect the target vocabulary cards and reshuffle them.
3. Introduce the cards one by one, identifying the terms correctly and incorrectly at random.
4. Model how to say Yes when the card is correctly identified, and No when it is incorrectly identified.

> **I:** "Doctor." (Hold up the **doctor** card.)
> **I:** "Doctor. Yes." (Point to the **doctor** card. Nod to indicate Yes. Motion for the learners to repeat.)
> **G:** "Yes."
> **I:** "Hospital." (Hold up the **doctor** card again.)
> **I:** "Hospital. No." (Point to the **doctor** card. Shake head to indicate No. Ask the learners to repeat.)
> **G:** "No."

5. Continue with other target vocabulary at random.
6. Repeat words as necessary until each word has been identified correctly.

Oral Language Activity 2

MATERIALS

Large vocabulary cards (from Lessons A & B, with multiple copies of selected cards from Lesson A)

Sorting activity sheet (one enlarged and one per learner)

Yarn

Review Target Nouns

1. Show each large vocabulary card to the group and have them identify each term.

> **I:** "What's this? (Hold up the **fever** card. Motion for a response.)
>
> **G:** "Fever."

2. Continue with the other vocabulary cards to ensure the group's familiarity with each term.
3. Put up the **doctor** card on one side of the board or on chart paper. Put the **hospital** and **ER** cards on the other side.
4. Separate the cards by drawing a line or using a piece of yarn to divide them into two columns.
5. Divide the vocabulary cards (from Lessons A and B) into two groups, **doctor** and **hospital/ER.**
6. Pair parts of the body with adjectives or the verb to create phrases as indicated below.
7. Hold up each card or two-card phrase and associate each with either the **doctor** or **hospital/ER** columns (see Adapting Lesson Activities, p. 28). If possible, elicit responses from learners. Put each card or phrase in the appropriate column.

Examples

Doctor	Hospital/ER
Cough	Broken arm
Stomach hurts	Broken leg
Ear hurts	Chest hurts
Eye hurts	Broken foot
Fever (100-102)	Fever (103+)
Hand cut	Hand burned
Throat hurts	
Back hurts	

8. Repeat terms and which location each belongs in before continuing on to the Sorting Activity.

Doctor or Hospital/ER Sorting Activity

1. Shuffle the large vocabulary cards (from Lessons A and B) and distribute them among the learners. Give learners individual cards or paired phrase cards (see examples on the following page).
2. Place the **doctor** and **hospital/ER** cards at the front of the room or in another visible location.

3. Have the learners take turns identifying the card(s) they each hold and placing the card(s) under **doctor** or **hospital/ER.**

> I: "What's this?" (Call on the learner holding the **broken** and **leg** cards. Point to the cards. Motion for a response from that learner.)
>
> L: "Broken leg." (Place the cards in the **hospital/ER** column.)

Examples

Doctor	Hospital/ER
Cough	Broken arm
Stomach hurts	Broken leg
Ear hurts	Chest hurts
Eye hurts	Broken foot
Fever (100-102)	Fever (103+)
Hand cut	Hand burned
Throat hurts	
Back hurts	

4. After all cards have been sorted, reshuffle the cards and distribute them among the learners, so that each learner has a different card or two-card phrase.
5. Repeat the sorting process as necessary to ensure the group's understanding of where they need to go for treatment of each medical problem according to the list above.

Comprehension Check

1. Distribute a Sorting activity sheet to each learner.
2. Post the enlarged copy of the activity sheet in the front of the room or in another visible location.
3. On the enlarged activity sheet, point to each picture or pair of pictures. Ask the learners to identify if the medical conditions pictured are for the doctor or the hospital emergency room to treat.
4. Model how to check the correct column on the activity sheet.
5. Have learners complete their own activity sheets by checking the correct column for each item.
6. Assist the group as necessary.

Oral Language Activity 3

MATERIALS

Large vocabulary cards
(from Lessons A & B)

Number cards for
100–103

OK/Not OK cards

Yes/No cards

Introduce the Target Question

1. Review the vocabulary from Lessons A and B by showing each of the vocabulary cards and eliciting a response from the group.

> **I:** "Who's this?" (Hold up the **doctor** card and motion for a response.)
>
> **G:** "Doctor."
>
> **I:** "Good. What's this?" (Hold up the **hospital** card. Motion for a response.)
>
> **G:** "Hospital."
>
> **I:** "Good. What's this?" (Hold up the **ER** card. Motion for a response.)
>
> **G:** "ER."

2. Assist learners by saying any terms that are not correctly identified and having learners repeat them.

3. Introduce all the vocabulary cards to ensure that learners know the terms.

4. Review phrases for medical problems by combining noun cards with adjective, verb, or number cards and eliciting a response from the group.

> **I:** "What's this?" (Hold up the **arm** and **broken** cards.)
>
> **G:** "Broken arm."

5. Post the **doctor** and the **hospital/ER** cards in the front of the room or in another visible location.

6. Hold up each noun card or two-card phrase (see examples, page 36). Ask learners the target question and elicit a response.

> **I:** "Where do you go?" (Hold up the **broken** and **arm** cards. Point to the **doctor** and the **hospital/ER** cards. Motion for the group to respond.)
>
> **G:** "Hospital ER."
>
> **I:** "Good. Where do you go?" (Hold up the **cough** card. Point to the **doctor** and the **hospital/ER** cards. Motion for a response.)
>
> **G:** "Doctor."

7. Continue asking the group to decide whether each medical problem listed below requires going to the doctor's office or going to the hospital emergency room. If possible, indicate mild or extreme cases of some of the conditions.

Examples

Doctor	Hospital/ER
Cough	Broken arm
Stomach hurts	Broken leg
Ear hurts	Chest hurts
Eye hurts	Broken foot
Fever (100-102)	Fever (103+)
Hand cut	Hand burned
Throat hurts	
Back hurts	

Concept Development Activity

1. Shuffle and distribute all of the vocabulary cards from Lessons A and B to the group. Include the number cards.
2. Post the **doctor** and the **hospital/ER** cards in the front of the room or in another visible location.
3. Have learners use single cards or pairs of cards to show various medical conditions (**broken leg, fever,** etc.). Learners can work together or trade to get the cards needed for a given medical problem.
4. Have each learner show and identify verbally a medical problem for the group.
5. Have each learner show his or her card(s) for the medical problem identified and respond to the target question by saying whether the problem should be treated at the doctor's office or at the hospital.

> **L:** "Broken arm." (Hold up the **broken** and **arm** cards.)
> **I:** "Where do you go?" (Point to the **doctor** and the **hospital/ER** cards. Motion for a response.)
> **L:** "Hospital ER."

6. Use the **OK** and **Not OK** cards to help guide learners into changing their answers if they are not correct.

> **L:** "Fever." (Hold up the **101** and **fever** cards.)
> **I:** "Where do you go?" (Point to the **doctor** and the **hospital/ER** cards. Motion for the learner to respond.)
> **L:** "Hospital ER."
> **I:** "Not OK." (Point to the **doctor** and the **hospital/ER** cards and motion for a response.)
> **L:** "Doctor."

Comprehension Check

1. Post the **Yes** and **No** cards at the front of the room or in another visible location.

2. Hold up vocabulary cards (single cards or combinations of cards) for various conditions. Identify whether the conditions should be treated at the doctor's office or at the hospital by holding up either the **hospital/ER** cards or the **doctor** card, giving correct or incorrect places of treatment at random.
3. Have learners say Yes or No and point to the **Yes** or **No** card to indicate if the place of treatment was correct or incorrect.
4. Model the responses for learners before having them respond independently.

> **I:** "Where do you go?" (Hold up the **broken** and **leg** cards. Hold up the **hospital/ER** cards. Nod head to indicate Yes. Motion for the group to choose the **Yes** card.)
>
> **G:** "Yes." (Point to the **Yes** card.)
>
> **I:** "Where do you go?" (Hold up the **hand** and **cut** cards. Hold up the **hospital/ER** cards. Shake head to indicate No. Motion for the group to choose the **No** card.)
>
> **G:** "No."

5. Make sure that various conditions and places of treatment (hospital/ER or doctor's office) are shown to check the group's understanding of where to go for treatment.

Oral Language Activity 4

MATERIALS

Large vocabulary cards (from Lessons A & B)

Number cards

Introduce the Dialogue

1. Review the sentence forms from Lesson A. Use **my** with parts of the body and adjective or verb cards to build sentences.

> **I:** "What's this?" (Hold up the **foot** card. Motion for a response.
>
> **G:** "Foot."
>
> **I:** "My foot." (Hold up the **foot** card. Point to your own foot. Motion for the learners to repeat.)
>
> **G:** "My foot." (Learners should point to their feet.)
>
> **I:** "Good. My foot." (Hold up the **foot** card. Point to your own foot. Motion for the learners to repeat.)
>
> **G:** "My foot." (Learners should point to their feet.)
>
> **I:** "What's this?" (Hold up the **cut** card. Motion for a response.)
>
> **G:** "Cut."
>
> **I:** "Yes. My foot is cut." (Hold up the **foot** and **cut** cards. Motion for learners to repeat.)
>
> **G:** "My foot is cut."
>
> **I:** "My head hurts." (Hold up the **head** and **hurts** cards. Motion for learners to repeat.)
>
> **G:** "My head hurts."

2. Use combinations of vocabulary cards to help learners review other sentences.
3. Hold up individual noun cards to help learners review terms for problems that do not fit the sentence patterns (e.g., **cough** and **fever**).
4. Write the model dialogue (see example below) on the board or on chart paper.
5. Read through the dialogue and point to each word.
6. Use vocabulary cards, mime, and gestures as appropriate to assist the group in understanding the dialogue.

Speaker 1:	"What's wrong?" (Hold up the **hurts** and **ear** cards. Motion for a response.)
Speaker 2:	"My ear hurts." (Point to the **hurts** and **ear** cards.)
Speaker 1:	"Where do you go?" (Hold up the **hospital/ER** and the **doctor** cards. Motion for a response.)
Speaker 2:	"Doctor." (Point to the **doctor** card.)
Speaker 1:	"What's wrong?" (Hold up the **broken** and **arm** cards. Motion for a response.)
Speaker 2:	"My arm is broken." (Point to the **broken** and **arm** cards.)
Speaker 1:	"Where do you go?" (Hold up the **hospital/ER** and the **doctor** cards. Motion for a response.)
Speaker 2:	"Hospital ER." (Point to the **hospital/ER** cards.)

7. Introduce the dialogue and have the group respond as Speaker 2. Ask the questions, prompt learners by holding up the appropriate noun and adjective or verb cards, and motion for a response.
8. Repeat the dialogue, substituting other nouns that go with the adjectives or verb.
9. Include nouns or phrases that do not use the full sentence patterns (e.g., **cough, fever** + number card) to practice with all the medical problems in the unit.

Dialogue Activity

1. Practice the dialogue (see example below) as a group, with learners responding to the instructor's verbal and visual prompts.
2. Use vocabulary cards to prompt learners to identify both medical problems and where to go for treatment.
3. Have the group repeat their response until they are able to say it in unison.

> **I:** "What's wrong?" (Hold up the **cut** and **hand** cards. Motion for a response.)
>
> **G:** "My hand is cut." (Learners should point to the **cut** and **hand** cards.)
>
> **I:** "Where do you go?" (Hold up the **hospital/ER** and the **doctor** cards. Motion for a response.)
>
> **G:** "Doctor." (Learners should hold up the **doctor** card.)
>
> **I:** "What's wrong?" (Hold up the **broken** and **arm** cards. Motion for a response.)
>
> **G:** "My arm is broken." (Learners should point to the **broken** and **arm** cards.)
>
> **I:** "Where do you go?" (Hold up the **hospital/ER** and the **doctor** cards. Motion for a response.)
>
> **G:** "Hospital ER." (Learners should hold up the **hospital/ER** cards.)

4. Perform the dialogue at least three times with the learners.
5. Repeat the dialogue using various combinations of cards to prompt different responses.

Comprehension Check

1. Place all of the vocabulary cards in a visible location and have the group respond to the questions, *What's wrong?* and *Where do you go?* Have learners point to the cards that correspond to their responses.
2. Encourage learners to use a full sentence if possible when responding to the question, *What's wrong?*

> **I:** "What's wrong?" (Mime having a stomachache. Motion for a response.)
>
> **G:** "My stomach hurts." (Learners should point to the **stomach** and **hurts** cards.)
>
> **I:** "Where do you go?" (Point to the **doctor** and the **hospital/ER** cards. Motion for a response.)
>
> **G:** "Doctor." (Learners should point to the **doctor** card.)

3. Substitute a variety of medical conditions and mime each one, having the group respond by pointing to the correct corresponding cards.
4. Have the group decide if the condition requires treatment at the hospital emergency room or at the doctor's office and respond with the correct term.

Reading Activity

MATERIALS

Large vocabulary cards (from Lessons A & B)

Circle the Correct Word activity sheet (one enlarged and one per learner)

Review

1. Shuffle the large vocabulary cards.
2. Show each card to the group while pronouncing each word slowly and clearly.
3. Run a finger under each word to help learners begin to recognize the words apart from the pictures.
4. Have the learners repeat the words at least three times.

> **I:** "Doctor." (Point to the word.)
>
> **G:** "Doctor."
>
> **I:** "Doctor." (Underline the word with a finger. Motion for the group to repeat the word.)
>
> **G:** "Doctor."

5. Continue to review with the cards, using the pattern above.
6. Fold cards in half to show only the words, to help learners become less dependent on the pictures.
7. Move from group to individual practice as learners become more comfortable reading the words without the assistance of the pictures.

NOTE

Separating words from pictures should be done gradually and after plenty of practice.

Circle the Correct Word Activity

1. Display the large vocabulary cards from Lessons A and B in a visible location for learners' reference.
2. Distribute a Circle the Correct Word activity sheet to each learner.
3. Post an enlarged activity sheet in the front of the room or in another visible location.
4. Using the enlarged activity sheet, ask learners to look at and identify each picture or pair of pictures.
5. Help learners to use the large vocabulary cards to match the picture(s) to one of the words or phrases listed next to the picture.
6. Show learners how to circle the word or phrase that corresponds to the picture(s) in each item.

> **I:** "Doctor." (Point to the picture of the doctor. Motion for learners to look at the vocabulary cards. Mime looking for the word **doctor**.)
>
> **I:** "Here it is. Doctor." (Circle the corresponding word on the enlarged activity sheet.)

7. Complete the activity sheet as a group.

Writing Activity

MATERIALS

Large vocabulary cards (from Lessons A & B)

Sort and Write activity sheet (one enlarged and one per learner)

NOTE

Separating words from pictures should be done gradually and after plenty of practice.

Review

1. Shuffle the large vocabulary cards.
2. Show each card to the group while pronouncing each word slowly and clearly.
3. Run a finger under each word to help learners begin to recognize the words apart from the pictures.
4. Have the learners repeat the words at least three times.

> **I:** "Doctor." (Point to the word.)
> **G:** "Doctor."
> **I:** "Doctor." (Underline the word with a finger. Motion for the group to repeat the word.)
> **G:** "Doctor."

5. Continue to review with the cards, using the pattern above.
6. Fold cards in half to show only the words, to help learners become less dependent on the pictures.
7. Move from group to individual practice as learners become more comfortable reading the words without the assistance of the pictures.

Sort and Write Activity

1. Display the large vocabulary cards from Lessons A and B in a visible location for learners' reference.
2. Distribute a Sort and Write activity sheet to each learner.
3. Post an enlarged copy of the activity sheet in the front of the room or in another visible location.
4. Use the enlarged activity sheet to demonstrate how to complete the activity. Point to a picture or pair of pictures on the sheet. Motion for learners to respond and also to identify whether the problem should be treated at the doctor's office or at the hospital.

> **I:** "What's wrong?" (Point to the pictures in the first item. Motion for learners to respond.)
> **G:** "Broken leg."
> **I:** "Where do you go?" (Point to the pictures of the doctor and the hospital at the top of each column.)
> **G:** "Hospital ER."

5. On the enlarged activity sheet, model writing the medical condition one word at a time on the line provided, in the correct column.

6. Have the group complete each column on their own activity sheets. Encourage learners to use the displayed vocabulary cards for reference.
7. Assist learners as necessary.

1

Unit Review Activity

MATERIALS

Unit Review activity sheet (one enlarged and one per learner)

Large vocabulary cards (from Lessons A & B)

NOTE

The Unit Review Activity can be done as a group activity for reinforcing the concepts learned in the lesson or done as an individual activity for assessment purposes.

Go to the Hospital Activity

1. Use the large vocabulary cards from Lessons A and B to review the vocabulary and concepts from the unit.
2. Hold up single cards or pairs of cards to indicate various medical conditions (see examples below). Have learners identify the conditions.

Examples

Cough	Broken arm
Stomach hurts	Broken leg
Ear hurts	Chest hurts
Eye hurts	Broken foot
Fever (100-102)	Fever (103+)
Hand cut	Hand burned
Throat hurts	
Back hurts	

3. Put the **hospital** and **ER** cards in the front of the room. For each medical condition, point to the card and ask learners if it is OK or Not OK to go to the hospital emergency room for that condition.
4. Distribute a copy of the Unit Review activity sheet to each learner. Post an enlarged copy of the activity sheet in the front of the room.
5. On the enlarged activity sheet, point to each combination of pictures. Have learners identify the condition.
6. Use the first item to show learners how to check OK or Not OK to indicate if they should go to the hospital emergency room for that condition.

I:	"What's this?" (Point to the first combination of pictures.)
G:	"Broken leg."
I:	"Where do you go?"
G:	"Hospital ER."
I:	"Good. Hospital ER. OK." (Motion for learners to repeat.)
G:	"Hospital ER. OK."

7. Demonstrate how to check the OK column for the first item.
8. Ask learners to complete the activity. If necessary, use the enlarged activity sheet to model checking the appropriate column for the other medical conditions.
9. Assist learners as necessary.

Central Theme Picture

Unit 1 *Using Doctor and Hospital Services* Lesson A *Life Skill*

Arm

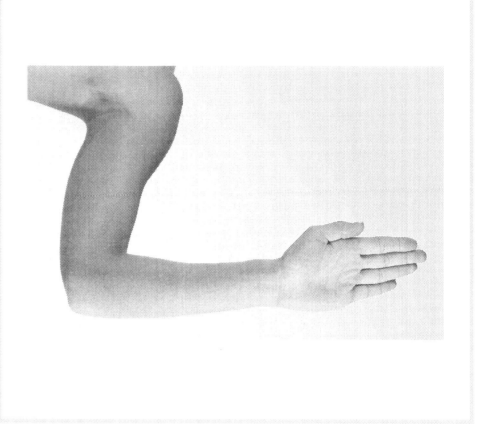

Chest

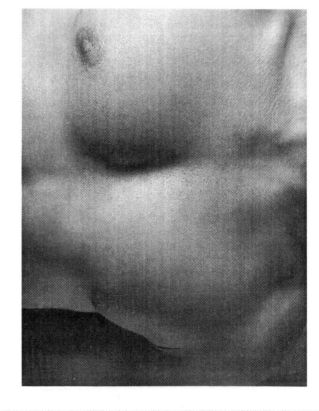

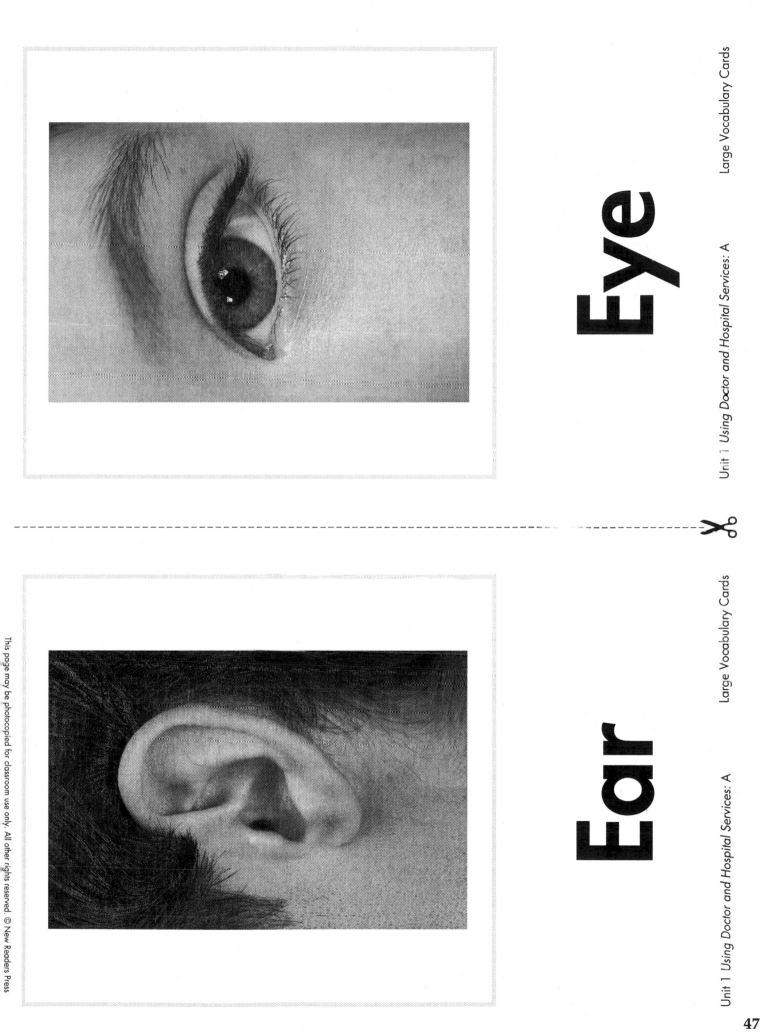

Eye

Ear

Foot

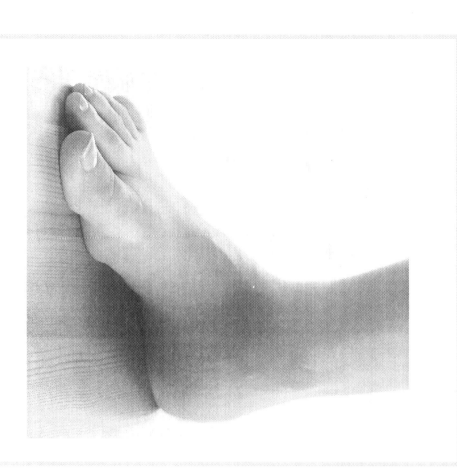

✂ -

Hand

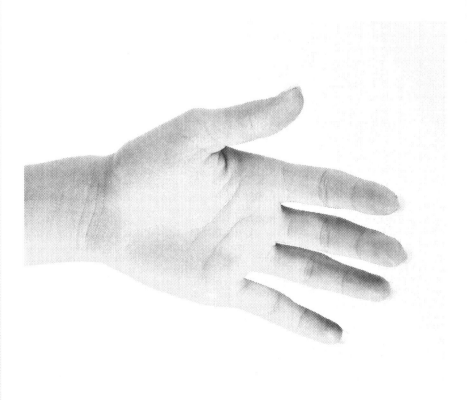

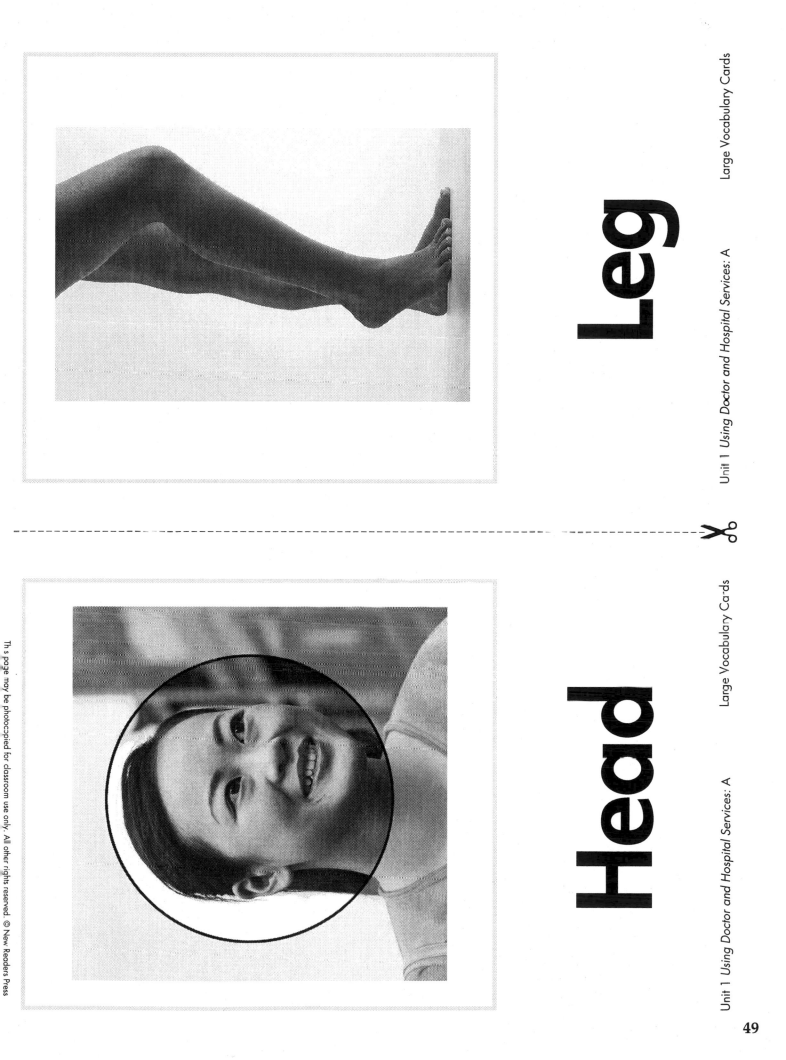

Leg

Unit 1 *Using Doctor and Hospital Services: A*

Head

Unit 1 *Using Doctor and Hospital Services: A*

Back

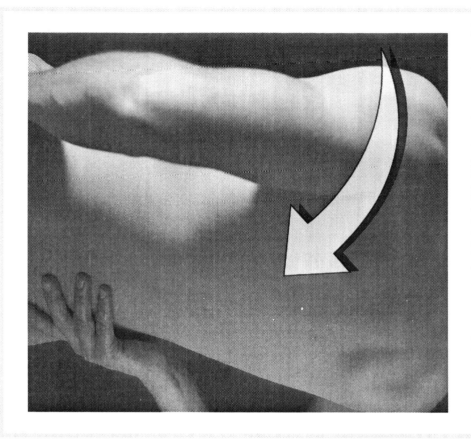

Throat

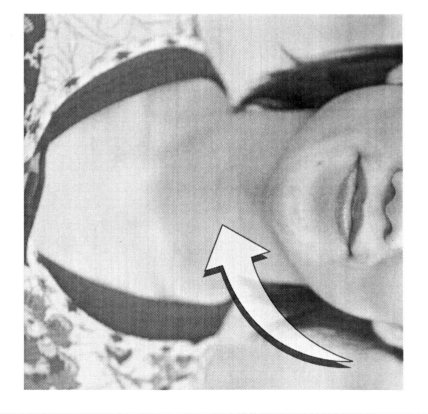

Stomach

Unit 1 *Using Doctor and Hospital Services:* A

Large Vocabulary Cards

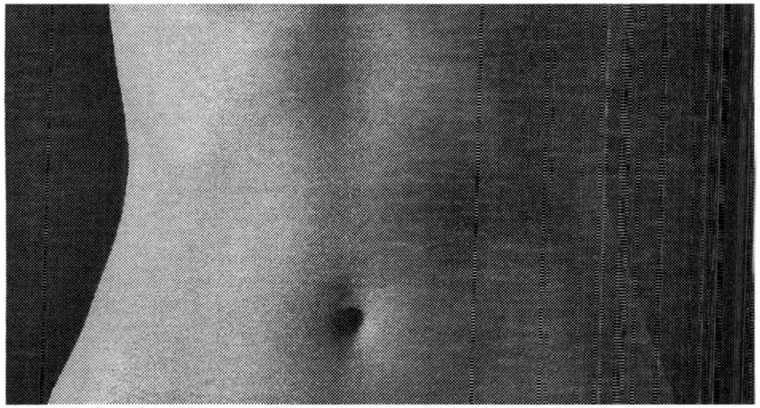

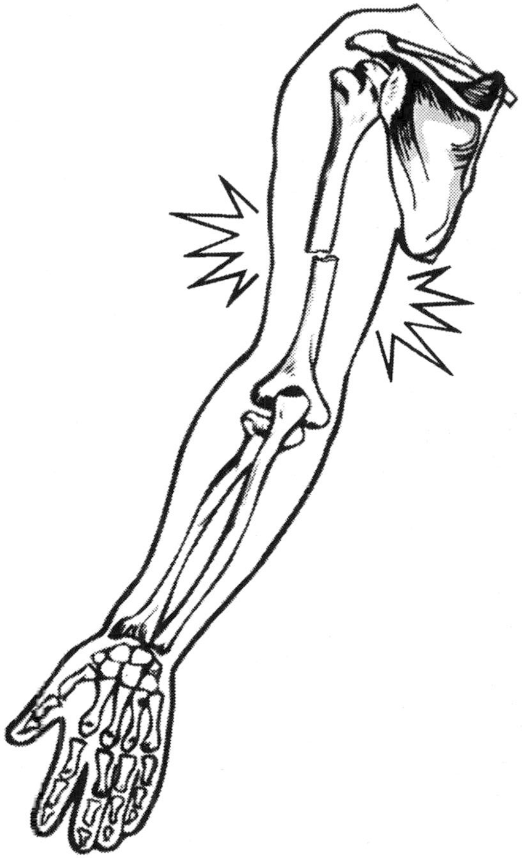

Broken

Unit 1 *Using Doctor and Hospital Services:* A

Large Vocabulary Cards

Burned

Cut

Yes

No

Hurts

Large Vocabulary Cards

Unit 1 *Using Doctor and Hospital Services: A*

Body Part Labeling Activity

Noun Spinner

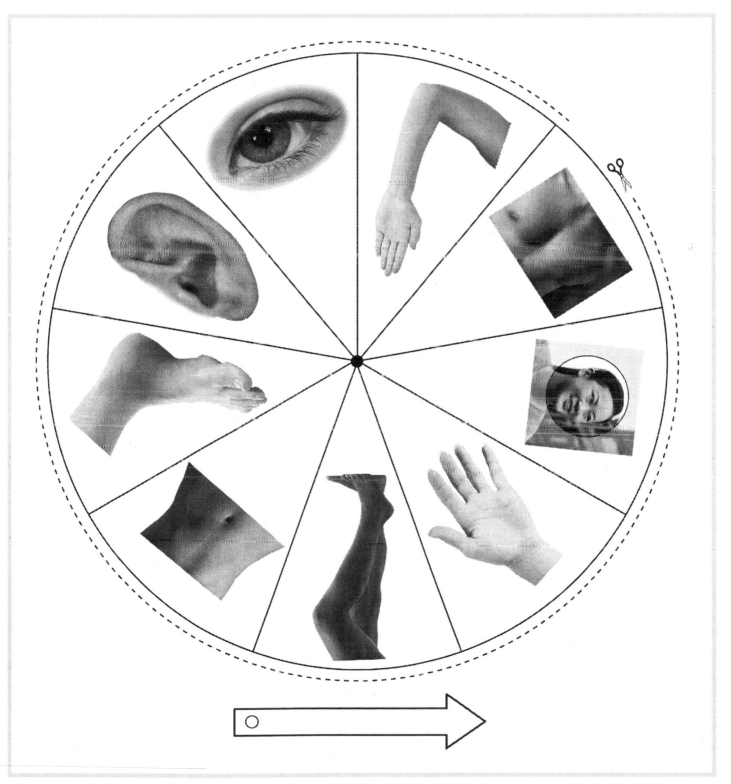

Unit 1 *Using Doctor and Hospital Services* Lesson A *Life Skill*

Noun Spinner

Adjectives and Verb Spinner

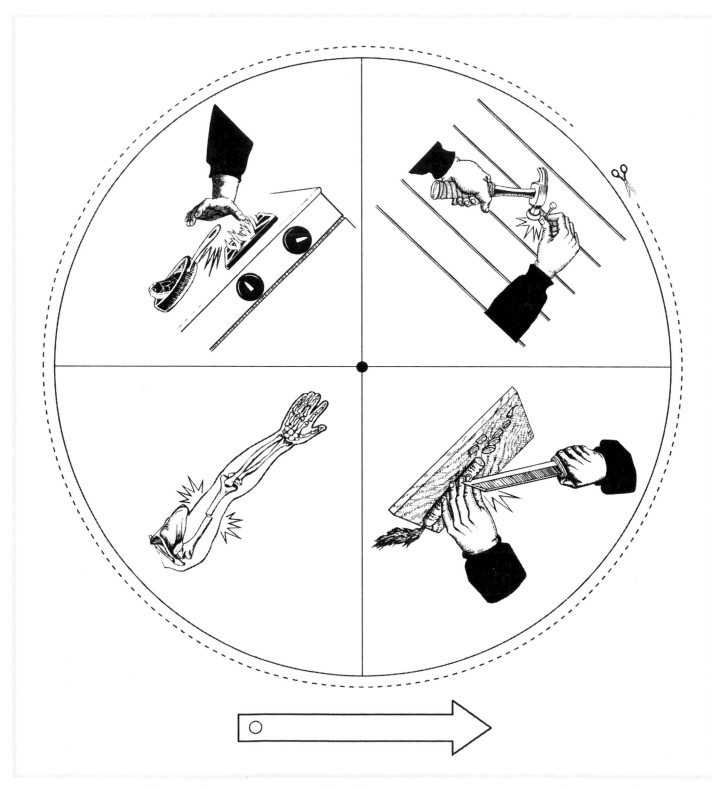

Unit 1 *Using Doctor and Hospital Services* Lesson A *Life Skill*

Adjectives and Verb Spinner

Word Search Activity

Use the pictures. Find the words in the puzzle. Circle the words.

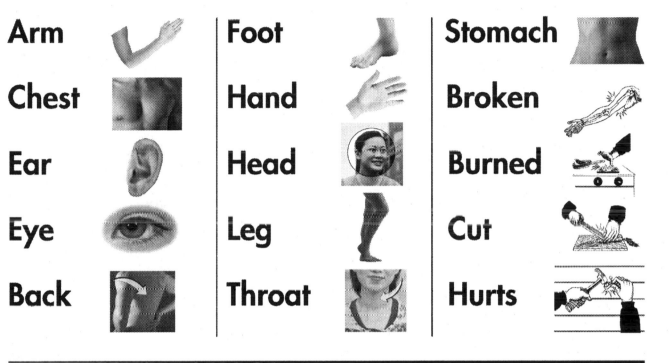

i	n	b	a	r	m	n	s	h	e	a	d	p	k	e
f	l	s	n	k	b	a	c	k	t	h	r	o	a	t
f	c	h	e	s	t	i	a	u	f	o	o	t	k	d
n	z	l	j	h	a	n	d	g	b	u	r	n	e	d
e	y	e	p	p	f	d	a	n	h	u	r	t	s	g
x	l	e	g	u	y	b	r	o	k	e	n	f	y	m
s	t	o	m	a	c	h	j	d	o	u	k	u	t	q
t	l	c	u	t	a	s	e	a	r	u	o	p	w	z

Label the Parts of the Body Activity

Label the parts of the body. Write on the lines.

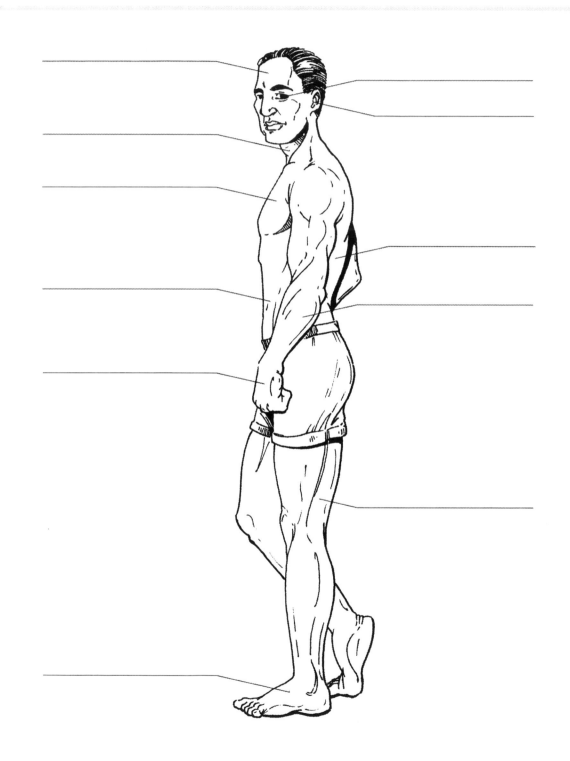

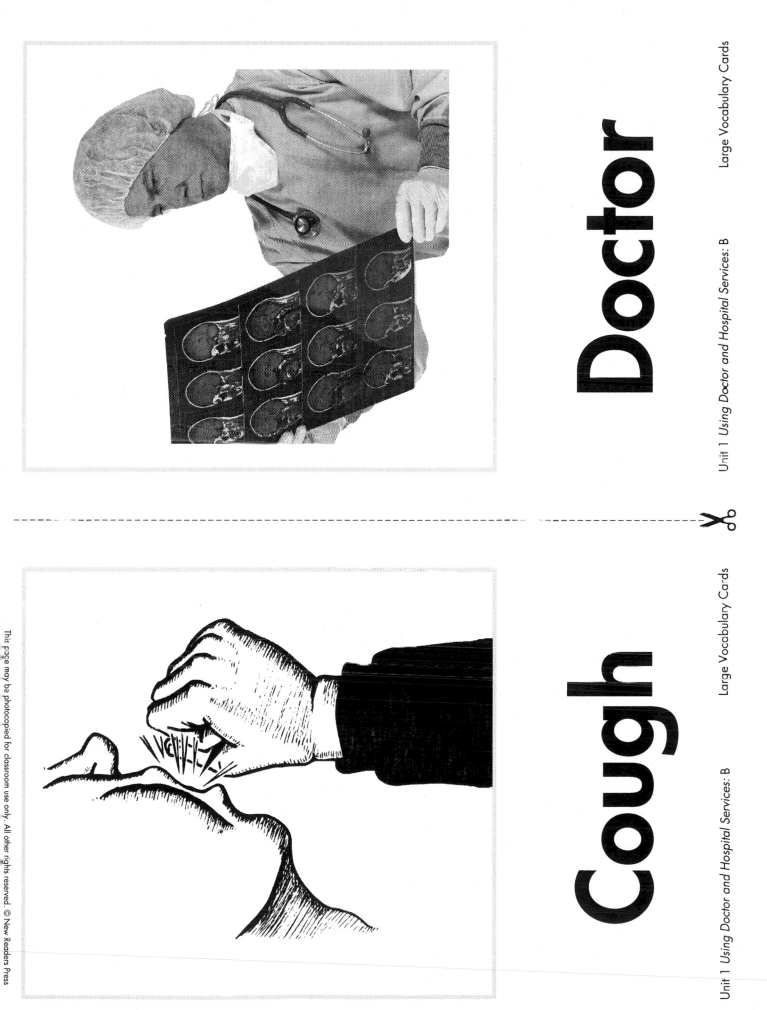

Doctor

Cough

Fever

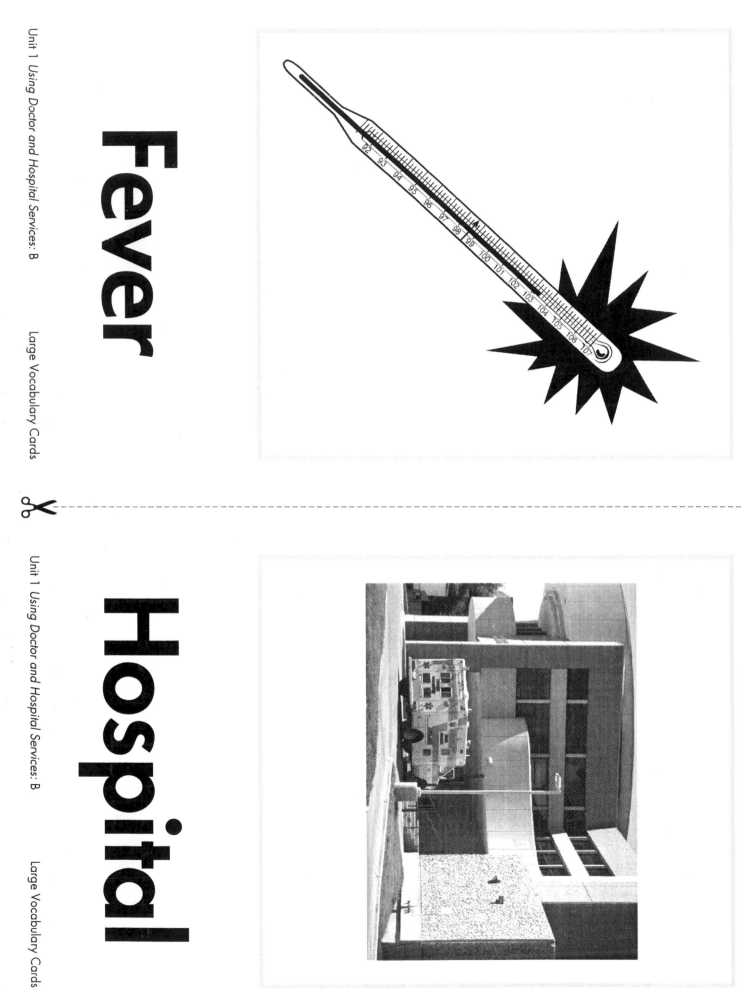

Hospital

ER
(Emergency room)

Unit 1 *Using Doctor and Hospital Services: B*   Large Vocabulary Cards

Sorting Activity

Check Doctor or Hospital for each set of pictures.

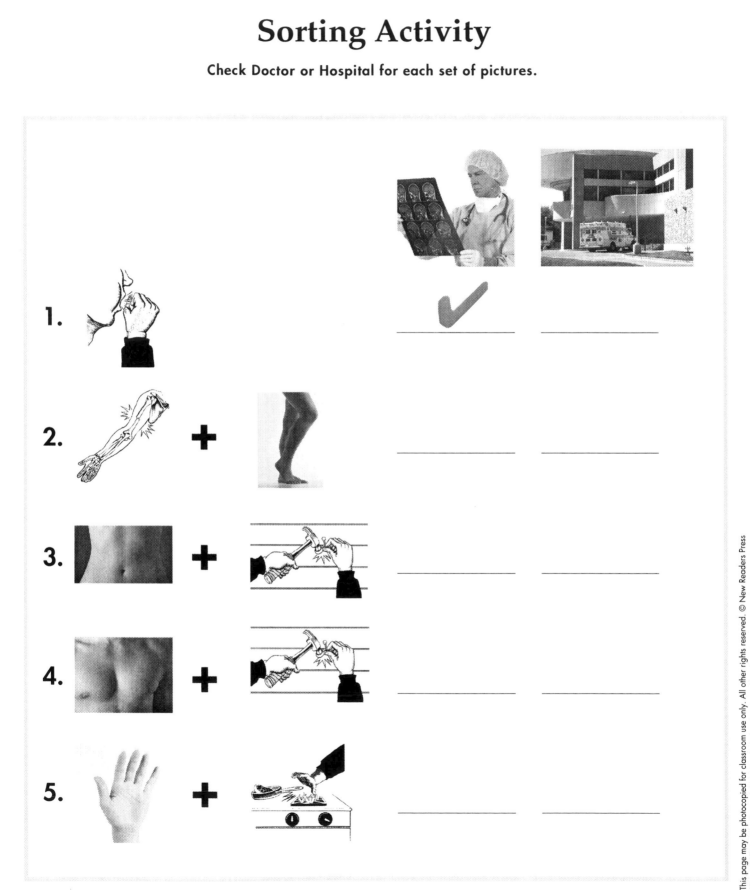

1.

2. +

3. +

4. +

5. +

Unit 1 *Using Doctor and Hospital Services* Lesson B *Civic Responsibility*

Activity Sheet

Circle the Correct Word Activity

Look at the pictures. Circle the correct words.

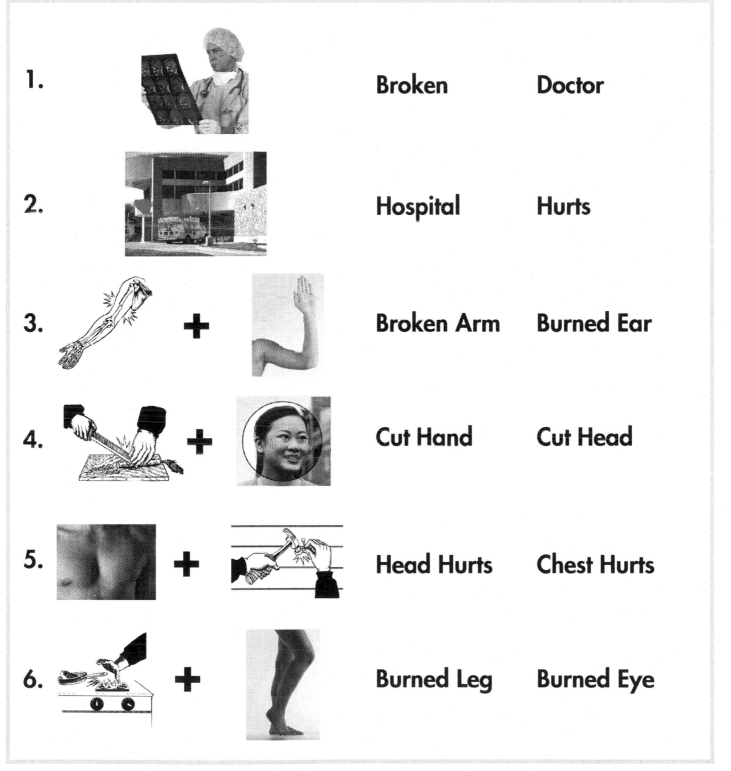

1. Broken   Doctor

2. Hospital   Hurts

3. Broken Arm   Burned Ear

4. Cut Hand   Cut Head

5. Head Hurts   Chest Hurts

6. Burned Leg   Burned Eye

Sort and Write Activity

Look at the pictures. Write the words under Doctor or Hospital.

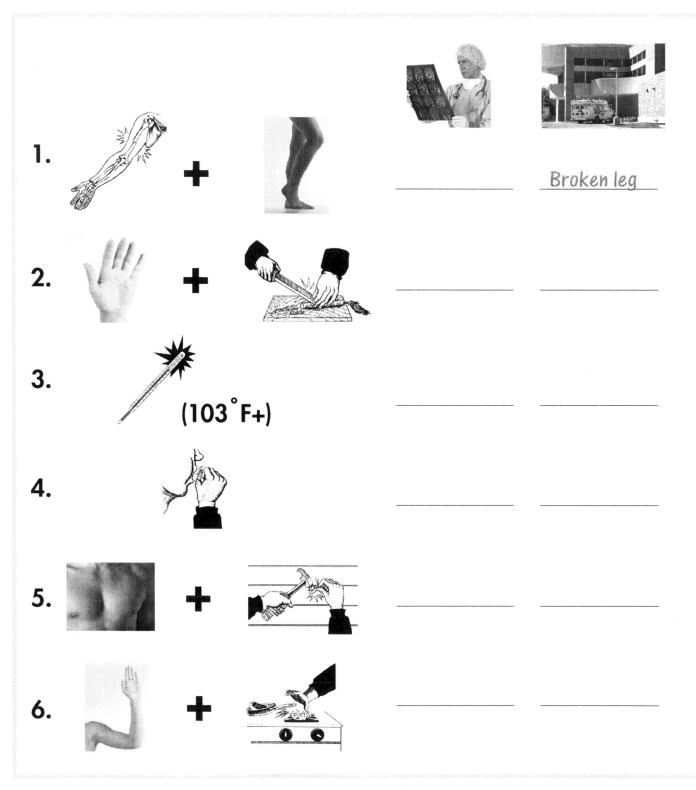

1. _____   Broken leg

2. _____   _____

3. (103°F+)   _____   _____

4. _____   _____

5. _____   _____

6. _____   _____

Unit 1 *Using Doctor and Hospital Services* Lesson B *Civic Responsibility*

Writing Activity Sheet

Go to the Hospital

Look at the pictures. Check OK if the hospital is OK for that condition.
Check Not OK if the hospital is Not OK for that condition.

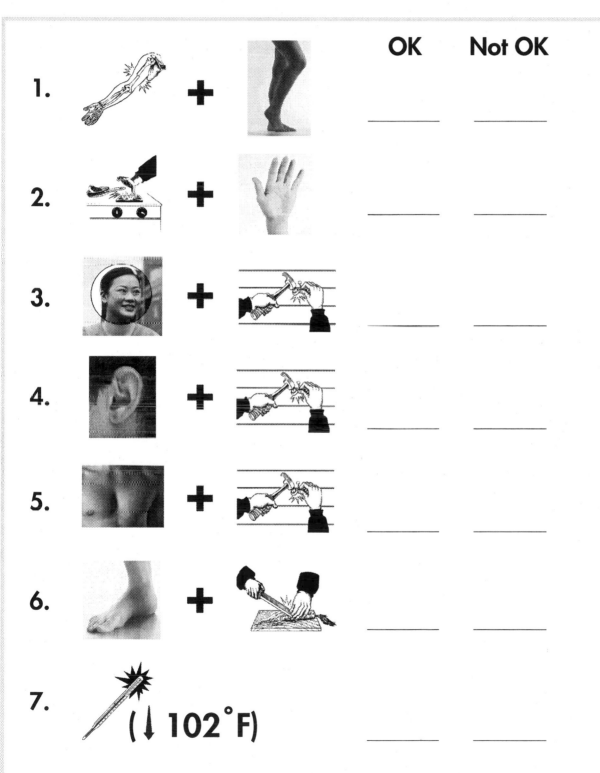

	OK	Not OK
1.	_____	_____
2.	_____	
3.	_____	_____
4.	_____	_____
5.	_____	_____
6.	_____	_____
7.	_____	_____

Handling Dangerous Chemicals

Safe Use of Chemicals

VOCABULARY

NOUNS

Chemicals

Pesticides

Plants

Shampoo

Soap

Soil

Water

Work clothes

VERBS & VERB PHRASES

Eat

Drink

Shower

Use toilet

Wash face

Wash hands

PREPOSITIONS

After

Before

Objectives

- To help learners understand basic safety information about pesticides and other dangerous chemicals
- To help learners understand some preventive measures to avoid chemical-related illnesses

Adapting Lesson Activities

Many non-English speaking adults, including newly arrived immigrants and migrant workers, have jobs that require direct handling of or other exposure to potentially dangerous chemicals, including pesticides. The vocabulary in this lesson, drawn largely from agricultural and landscape work and the risks of pesticide exposure, can easily be adapted and expanded to meet the needs of learners in janitorial, industrial, or other jobs that involve handling potentially dangerous chemicals. Find out about learners' jobs and the specific safety precautions appropriate for workers in those jobs. Then identify pictures and/or realia representing additional or alternative vocabulary to present and practice in the lesson activities.

Materials Included

- Central theme picture
- Large reproducible vocabulary cards
- **Before/After** cards
- Concept Development cards
- Die pattern
- Small word strips to attach to the die
- Sentence Completion activity sheet
- **Yes/No** cards
- **OK/Not OK** cards (page 208)

Materials Needed

- A calendar
- A real or instructor-made picture of a clock (analog version)
- Additional instructor copy (enlarged) of the activity sheet
- Die, coin, or other instructor-devised method to use as a counter
- Buttons, coins, or various small objects to use as place markers
- Pictures and/or real objects to show chemicals or processes using chemicals for jobs familiar to learners.

Central Theme Picture

MATERIALS

Theme picture

NOTE

Many warning signs in the U.S. are in English and Spanish. Point this out to students from language backgrounds other than English or Spanish, so they realize why the words may not look familiar.

POSSIBLE RESPONSES

Chemical	Sign
Man	Field
Poison	Point
Danger	Spray
Plant	

Introduce the Theme Picture

1. Show learners the theme picture and ask for a response.
2. Encourage learners to say anything about the picture that they can.

> **I:** "What's happening in this picture?" (Point out key things about the picture to elicit a response.)

Oral Language Activity 1

MATERIALS

Large noun cards

Introduce the Target Nouns

1. Show each large noun card to the group while pronouncing each word slowly and clearly.

> **I:** "Plants." (Hold up the **plants** card. Motion for the group to repeat together.)
> **G:** "Plants."
> **I:** "Good. Plants." (Motion for the group to repeat.)
> **G:** "Plants."
> **I:** "Plants." (Motion for the group to repeat. Put the **plants** card at the front of the room.)
> **G:** "Plants."

2. Introduce the remaining words using the format above.
3. Say each word and have the group repeat each one three times.
4. Repeat any words more than three times as necessary.
5. If learners have difficulty saying three-syllable words **(chemicals, pesticides),** break the word into parts and gradually help them build up to saying the whole word. In particular, help learners with pronunciation of the vowels. It may also help to model and have learners clap or beat out the stress pattern in the words.

Concentration

1. Place each card facedown on a table or other visible surface, making sure the cards do not overlap.
2. Turn over one card and identify it for the group or have learners identify it.
3. Demonstrate the activity by turning over another card in search of a matched pair.
4. Model getting a matched pair to show how a player with a matched pair keeps the cards and is allowed an extra turn.
5. Model getting cards that do not match to show how those cards must be put back facedown on the table.
6. Show the learners one success and one failure of finding a matched pair to help them understand the purpose of the activity.
7. Motion for the learners to begin the activity by choosing the first person to start.
8. Encourage learners to identify both cards verbally as they are selected.
9. Have learners again say which pairs they collected when the activity is finished.
10. Motion for the learners to hold up the pairs to show the group as they identify them.
11. Count each learner's pairs, and encourage the group to count along.
12. Hold the cards that are difficult for the group until the end of the activity and repeat them.
13. Assist learners as needed.

Comprehension Check

1. Shuffle both sets of vocabulary cards used in Oral Language Activity 1.
2. Place all of the cards faceup on a table or other visible surface.
3. Call out a term and ask the group to point to the correct cards. There will be two cards for each term.
4. Continue calling out terms at random. Encourage learners to find both cards for each term.
5. Repeat as necessary to ensure the group's comprehension of the terms.

Oral Language Activity 2

MATERIALS

Large vocabulary cards

Before/After cards

A calendar

A clock (analog)

Concept Development cards

OK/Not OK cards

Pictures and/or realia showing chemicals or use of chemicals

Introduce the Target Verb Phrases and Prepositions

1. Show each large verb card to the group, pronouncing each word slowly and clearly.

> **I:** "Eat." (Hold up the **eat** card. Motion for the group to repeat together.)
>
> **G:** "Eat."
>
> **I:** "Good. Eat." (Motion for the group to repeat.)
>
> **G:** "Eat."
>
> **I:** "Eat." (Motion for the group to repeat. Put the **eat** card at the front of the room.)
>
> **G:** "Eat."

2. Introduce the remaining verbs, using the format above.
3. Mime the action for each to reinforce meaning. Encourage learners to mime the actions as they repeat the verbs.
4. Show each large preposition card to the group, pronouncing each word slowly and clearly.
5. Use a calendar and a clock to help the group understand the concepts of **before** and **after.**
6. Say each word and have the group repeat each one three times.
7. Repeat any words more than three times as necessary.

Concept Development Activity

1. Hold up the **pesticides** card (as in the example below) and/or the **chemicals** card to show the group. Have the group identify it.
2. Use the **plants** card to show how pesticides may be used for agricultural or landscaping purposes, i.e., may be applied to plants. Use realia or pictures related to jobs that learners are familiar with to show appropriate uses of chemical products (e.g., cleaning supplies, pictures of industrial processes).
3. Have the group associate these selected uses with being OK.

> **I:** "Pesticides." (Hold up the **pesticides** card. Motion for the group to repeat together.)
>
> **G:** "Pesticides."
>
> **I:** "Pesticides on plants. OK." (Hold up the **pesticides, plants,** and **OK** cards. Motion for the group to repeat.)
>
> **G:** "Pesticides on plants. OK."

4. Show how pesticides or chemicals are Not OK when combined with water, soil, and work clothes if the water is used for drinking or work clothes are not washed. Show how chemicals (vapors) in the air can be Not OK on the skin or in the eyes, especially if there is limited ventilation.

5. Use the Concept Development cards to help learners understand what is OK and Not OK when using pesticides or chemicals.

Example Scenarios

Spraying crops = OK
Work clothes with long sleeves/long pants = OK
Washing work clothes and other clothes together = Not OK
Shower with soap and shampoo = OK
Eating without washing = Not OK
Washing hands and face before using the toilet = OK
Short sleeves/not using work clothes = Not OK

NOTE

The vocabulary and concept development cards and realia to indicate **after** can be used here to remind learners about also washing hands after using the toilet, for personal hygiene.

6. Use the **after** card and appropriate verb cards to emphasize to learners that it is necessary to wash their faces and hands and/or shower after exposure to pesticides or after using chemicals.

Comprehension Check

1. Hold up two Concept Development cards for the group.
2. Make sure that the learners can see both cards clearly.
3. Say *OK* or *Not OK* and have the learners point to the corresponding card.
4. Have the learners point to both cards if they are both categorized as OK or Not OK.

I: "OK." (Hold up the **spraying crops** and the **eating without washing** cards. Motion for a response.)

G: "OK." (Learners should point to the **spraying crops** card.)

I: "Not OK." (Hold up the **washing clothes together** and the **short sleeves** card. Motion for a response.)

G: "Not OK." (Learners should point to both the **washing clothes together** and the **short sleeves** cards.)

Oral Language Activity 3

MATERIALS

Large vocabulary cards

Safety activity board

A die, coin, or other counter

Place markers (one per learner)

OK/Not OK cards

NOTE

If a coin is being used as a counter, heads = move two spaces and tails = move one space.

This game can be used as is with learners who work with chemicals other than pesticides, since the principles of what is OK or Not OK will be very similar. If possible, replace some of the pictures and the terms with items that relate specifically to learners' jobs and experiences.

Review the Target Vocabulary

1. Hold up each large vocabulary card and motion for the group to respond.

> **I:** "What's this?" (Hold up the **wash hands** card. Motion for a response.)
>
> **G:** "Wash hands."
>
> **I:** "Good. What's this?" (Hold up the **shower** card. Motion for a response.)
>
> **G:** "Shower."

2. Use the method above to review other target vocabulary (nouns and verbs) with the group.
3. Encourage learners to mime the action on a verb card to reinforce understanding of the meaning.
4. If necessary while showing the vocabulary cards, mime the actions on the verb cards to give learners an additional prompt.
5. Assist learners as necessary.

Safety Activity

1. Give each learner a unique place marker. Put the place markers on START on the Safety activity board.
2. Give the die, coin, or other counter to a learner to begin the game. Guide learners through the game process, as in the example below.

> **I:** "OK. Please start." (Motion for the learner to roll the die or flip the coin.)
>
> **I:** "Great. Move two spaces." (Guide the learner to the correct place on the board. Motion for the learner to identify the picture.)
>
> **L:** "Wash clothes."
>
> **I:** "OK or Not OK?" (Motion to the learner for a response.)
>
> **L:** "OK."
>
> **I:** "Good work." (Motion for the next learner to take a turn.)

3. Have learners take turns and move around the board.
4. Ask learners to identify each scenario and indicate what is OK or Not OK.
5. Assist individuals as needed.

Comprehension Check

1. Hold up two cards. Identify one correctly.
2. Have the group point to the card that was identified, to demonstrate understanding.

3. Continue holding up other pairs of cards, combining cards at random. Mix cards and repeat to ensure comprehension of the terms.
4. Assist learners as necessary.

Oral Language Activity 4

MATERIALS

Large vocabulary cards

Introduce the Dialogue

1. Write the sample dialogue (see example below) on the board or on chart paper and read it for the group, pointing to each word.
2. Place the large vocabulary cards in a visible location at the front of the room to use as prompts for the dialogue. Use the **chemicals** card in place of the **pesticides** card in the example below if appropriate for learners' needs.

Speaker 1:	"What should you do?" (Hold up the **pesticides** card. Hold up the **work clothes** card. Motion for a response.)
Speaker 2:	"Wash work clothes."
Speaker 1:	"What should you do?" (Hold up the **pesticides** card. Hold up the **shower, soap,** and **shampoo** cards. Motion for a response.)
Speaker 2:	"Shower with soap and shampoo."
Speaker 1:	"What should you do?" (Hold up the **pesticides** card. Hold up the **wash face** card. Motion for response.)
Speaker 2:	"Wash face."
Speaker 1:	"What should you do?" (Hold up the **pesticides** card. Hold up the **wash hands** card. Motion for a response.)
Speaker 2:	"Wash hands."

NOTE

Pointing to each word while reading is important to do even if the learners are non-readers or nonliterate.

3. Point to each word whenever the dialogue is repeated in this activity.
4. Introduce the dialogue by assuming the role of Speaker 1 and having the group respond as Speaker 2.

Dialogue Activity

1. Write the sample dialogue (see example on the next page) on the board or on chart paper and read it for the group, pointing to each word.
2. Practice the dialogue, with the group responding to instructor's verbal and visual prompts. Use the **chemicals** card in place of the **pesticides** card in the following example if appropriate for learners' needs.

Speaker 1:	"What should you do?" (Hold up the **pesticides** card. Hold up the **work clothes** card. Motion for a response.)
Speaker 2:	"Wash work clothes."
Speaker 1:	"What should you do?" (Hold up the **pesticides** card. Hold up the **shower, soap,** and **shampoo** cards. Motion for a response.)
Speaker 2:	"Shower with soap and shampoo."
Speaker 1:	"What should you do?" (Hold up the **pesticides** card. Hold up the **wash face** card. Motion for a response.)
Speaker 2:	"Wash face."
Speaker 1:	"What should you do?" (Hold up the **pesticides** card. Hold up the **wash hands** card. Motion for a response.)
Speaker 2:	"Wash hands."

3. Point to each word whenever the dialogue is repeated in this activity.
4. Perform the dialogue as a group three times with the instructor assuming the role of Speaker 1 and the group responding as Speaker 2. Use the vocabulary cards as necessary to dramatize the dialogue.
5. Assist learners as needed.

Comprehension Check

1. Shuffle the large vocabulary cards and place them faceup on the table.
2. Call out a target noun or verb and motion for the group to pick up the corresponding card.
3. Ask the learner who picks up the correct card first to repeat the noun or verb.
4. Continue calling out target vocabulary until all of the cards have been collected.
5. Repeat the Comprehension Check, laying the cards out in different positions, to provide additional review.

Reading Activity

MATERIALS

Large vocabulary cards

Die pattern

Small word strips to attach to the die (dice)

Review

1. Shuffle all of the target vocabulary cards.
2. Show each card to the group while pronouncing each word slowly and clearly.
3. Run a finger under each word to help learners begin to recognize the words apart from the pictures.
4. Have the learners repeat the phrases at least three times.

> **I:** "Pesticides." (Point to the word.)
>
> **G:** "Pesticides."
>
> **I:** "Pesticides." (Underline the word with a finger. Motion for the group to repeat the word.)
>
> **G:** "Pesticides."

NOTE

Separating words from the pictures should be done gradually and after plenty of practice.

5. Continue to review with the cards, using the pattern above.
6. Fold cards in half to show only the words, to help learners become less dependent on the pictures.
7. Move from group to individual practice as learners become more comfortable reading the words without the assistance of the pictures.

Reading Dice Activity

NOTE

Create strips with alternative vocabulary words drawn from learners' jobs to use on the sides of the die for more reading practice.

1. Cut and fold the box outline to make a die. Attach the small word strips to each side of the die.
2. Prepare more than one die for a larger group, so that the group can be split up or two dice can be rolled at once.
3. Have the group form a circle.
4. Place the large vocabulary cards in a visible location for the learners to use for reference.
5. Demonstrate the activity by rolling the die (or one of multiple dice). Point to and identify the word that is displayed faceup on the die.
6. Have each learner, going around the circle, take a turn to roll and identify the word displayed faceup on the die from his or her roll, as in the example below.

> **I:** "OK. Roll. What's that?" (Motion to the learner that rolled the die to answer.)
>
> **L:** "Wash hands."
>
> **I:** "Good. OK. Next person." (Motion for the next person in the circle to roll and identify.)

7. Repeat, with different words attached to the sides of the die to practice reading all vocabulary words.

Writing Activity

MATERIALS

Large vocabulary cards

Sentence Completion activity sheet (one enlarged and one per learner)

Review

1. Shuffle all of the target vocabulary cards.
2. Show each card to the group while pronouncing each word slowly and clearly.
3. Run a finger under each word to help learners begin to recognize the words apart from the pictures.
4. Have the learners repeat the phrases at least three times.

> **I:** "Eat." (Point to the word.)
> **G:** "Eat."
> **I:** "Eat." (Underline the word with a finger. Motion for the group to repeat the word.)
> **G:** "Eat."

NOTE

Separating words from the pictures should be done gradually and after plenty of practice.

5. Continue to review with the cards, using the pattern above.
6. Fold cards in half to show only the words, to help learners become less dependent on the pictures.
7. Move from group to individual practice as learners become more comfortable reading the words without the assistance of the pictures.

Sentence Completion Activity

1. Distribute a Sentence Completion activity sheet to each learner.
2. Place an enlarged copy of the activity sheet in the front of the room or in another visible location.
3. On the enlarged activity sheet, point to each picture in turn and ask learners to identify the pictures.
4. Model each complete sentence for the group, pointing to the pictures and words in turn while reading.
5. Demonstrate how to complete the activity sheet by showing learners where to write the words corresponding to the pictures.
6. Have the learners write the correct word(s) under each picture.
7. Encourage learners to refer to the large vocabulary cards for assistance.

> **I:** "Work clothes are OK." (Point to the picture. Ask the group to respond.)
>
> **G:** "Work clothes are OK."
>
> **I:** "Work clothes are OK." (Show learners where the words should be written and have them use the vocabulary cards for assistance.)
>
> **I:** "What's this?" (Point to the **wash hands** picture and motion for a response.)
>
> **G:** "Wash hands."
>
> **I:** "Wash hands." (Show learners where the words should be written and have them use the vocabulary cards for assistance.)

8. Have volunteers come to the front of the room and complete the enlarged activity sheet by writing the correct words on the lines under the pictures. Alternatively, write the words on the enlarged activity sheet as learners identify the missing words.
9. Have learners complete the sentences on their own sheets.
10. Review by running a finger under each word and have learners read the completed sentences.

Lesson B - Civic Responsibility

Working with Dangerous Chemicals

VOCABULARY

NOUNS

Fresh water

Protective clothing

Sink

Toilet

Towel

Warning label

Warning sign

SENTENCE

I need (to) _____.

Objective

To make learners aware of their rights regarding pesticide or chemical use and exposure

Adapting Lesson Activities

The vocabulary in this lesson, again drawn largely from agricultural and landscape work and the risks of pesticide exposure, can easily be adapted and expanded to meet the needs of learners in janitorial, industrial, or other jobs that involve handling potentially dangerous chemicals. An understanding of learners' jobs and the specific safety precautions appropriate for workers in those jobs can help you identify pictures and/or realia representing additional or alternative vocabulary to present and practice in the lesson activities.

Materials Included

- Large reproducible vocabulary cards
- Comprehension Check activity sheet
- Picture/Word Matching activity sheet
- Label the Pictures activity sheet
- **OK/Not OK** cards (page 208)

Materials Needed

- Additional instructor copy (enlarged) of the activity sheets
- Pictures of a sink, a toilet, and a towel
- Real examples of protective clothing (appropriate to learners' jobs)
- Real or instructor-made replicas of warning signs and labels
- Yarn or string

Civics Introduction

Rights of Pesticide Users

Pesticides are strong chemicals which are applied to plants to destroy insects and weeds as well as prevent diseases that might impair plant growth and production. When handled improperly, pesticides are very dangerous to humans. Agricultural workers and other individuals working with pesticides, such as landscape workers, should be trained in safety measures for the application and handling of pesticides. Without proper safety precautions, pesticides can be inhaled, absorbed, or ingested. Serious health implications may result for individuals who have been directly contaminated as well as for those who have contact with contaminated clothing, skin, water, or other materials.

According to the Occupational Safety & Health Administration (OSHA), employers in the agricultural industry whose employees are working with pesticides must provide toilets and sinks with clean water within a quarter mile from the work location. Training on pesticide handling must be provided by employers and include the following:

- information about the types and names of pesticides used
- safety precautions for proper handling of pesticides
- contamination and poisoning symptoms
- information about emergency treatment

Warning signs with re-entry dates must also be placed in all areas where pesticides have been applied.

This topic is important for newly arrived, non-English-speaking adults as they may work in areas where pesticides have been used or are being used. Agricultural workers and other individuals should know their rights and take certain precautions to keep themselves safe from improper exposure to hazardous chemicals such as pesticides. Protective clothing should be worn in any area where pesticides have been used and pesticide-contaminated ground water should not be used for washing or drinking. If contact is made with contaminated water, soil, or the pesticide itself, the employee should immediately wash with soap and shampoo using fresh water. Any employee working with pesticides should also wash his or her hands and face before using the bathroom, eating, drinking, or smoking. Clothing exposed to pesticides should be washed in hot water, separate from other clothing. When washing cannot be done immediately, keeping protective clothing outside of the home in plastic bags, away from children and other family members, is also a safe practice.

Agricultural workers or other individuals who work with pesticides may consider contacting a local legal service provider if they believe that an employer is not in compliance with OSHA regulations for proper pesticide use.

Oral Language Activity 1

MATERIALS

Large noun cards
(two sets)

Pictures of a sink, a
toilet, and a towel

Real examples of
protective clothing and
warning signs

Introduce the Target Vocabulary

1. Hold up each noun card and motion for the learners to repeat each word.

> **I:** "Fresh water." (Hold up the **fresh water** card. Motion for the learners to repeat.)
>
> **G:** "Fresh water."
>
> **I:** "Fresh water." (Hold up the **fresh water** card. Mime turning on a faucet and filling a glass of water. Motion for the learners to repeat.)
>
> **G:** "Fresh water."
>
> **I:** "Fresh water." (Hold up the **fresh water** card. Motion for the learners to repeat.)
>
> **G:** "Fresh water."

2. Introduce all of the noun cards using the method above.
3. Use realia, mime, or gestures when necessary to clarify the meaning of terms.
4. Have the learners repeat each word at least three times.

NOTE

Photocopying each
set of noun cards on a
different color of paper
will help facilitate the
successful matching of
pairs. The learner who
collects the most pairs
wins.

Concentration

1. Shuffle two sets of large noun cards.
2. Place each card facedown on a table or other visible surface, making sure the cards do not overlap.
3. Turn over one card and identify it for the group.
4. Demonstrate the activity by turning over another card in search of a matched pair.
5. Model getting a matched pair to show how a player with a matched pair keeps the cards and is allowed an extra turn.
6. Model getting cards that do not match to show how those cards must be put back facedown on the table.
7. Show the learners one success and one failure of finding a matched pair, to help them understand the purpose of the activity.
8. Encourage learners to identify both cards verbally as they are selected.
9. Motion for learners to begin the activity by choosing the first person to start.
10. Have each learner choose two cards and identify the nouns.
11. Motion for the learners to hold up the pairs or cards to show the group as they identify them.
12. Count each learner's pairs or cards, and encourage the group, to count along when the activity is finished.

13. Hold the cards that are difficult for the group until the end of the activity and repeat them.
14. Assist learners as needed.

Comprehension Check

1. Hold up two cards. Identify one correctly.
2. Have the group point to the card that was identified, to demonstrate understanding.

> **I:** "Fresh water." (Hold up the **fresh water** and **protective clothing** cards. Motion for learners to choose the correct card.)
>
> **G:** "Fresh water." (Point to the card.)

3. Continue holding up other pairs of cards, combining cards at random. Mix cards and repeat to ensure comprehension of the terms.
4. Assist learners as necessary.

Oral Language Activity 2

MATERIALS

Large vocabulary cards

Introduce the Target Sentence Pattern

1. Hold up a noun or verb card (from Lessons A and B) representing something that helps limit pesticide or chemical exposure or contamination (**shampoo, soap, towel, work clothes, fresh water, protective clothing, wash clothes, shower, wash hands,** and **wash face**).
2. Motion for the learners to listen to the model of the target sentence and repeat the sentence.

> **I:** "I need fresh water." (Hold up the **fresh water** card. Point to yourself. Motion for the learners to repeat the term.)
>
> **G:** "I need fresh water."
>
> **I:** "I need fresh water." (Hold up the **fresh water** card. Mime turning on a faucet and filling a glass of water. Offer the imaginary glass to a learner in the room. Motion for the learners to repeat the term.)
>
> **G:** "I need fresh water."
>
> **I:** "I need fresh water." (Hold up the **fresh water** card. Point to yourself. Motion for the learners to repeat the term.)
>
> **G:** "I need fresh water."

3. Continue to teach the target sentence, substituting the other nouns. Model use of **a** where necessary for count nouns (e.g., I need a towel). For the appropriate verbs, use the pattern **I need to** (e.g., I need to wash clothes).
4. Use realia, mime, or gestures when necessary to clarify meaning.
5. Have the learners repeat the sentences three times.
6. Review the remaining nouns from Lesson A (**pesticides, plants, soil,** and **water**) by holding up the cards and having learners identify each one.

Pesticide Situations Activity

1. Hold up the **pesticides** card and have the learners identify the term.

> **I:** "What's this?" (Hold up the **pesticides** card and motion for the group to identify the term verbally.)
> **G:** "Pesticides."

2. Display the card in a visible location.
3. Hold up the **plants, soil, water,** and **work clothes** cards for the group to identify.

> **I:** "What's this?" (Hold up the **soil** card. Motion for the group to identify it verbally.)
> **G:** "Soil."
> **I:** "What's this?" (Hold up the **work clothes** card. Motion for the group to identify the term verbally.)
> **G:** "Work clothes."

4. Place each of these cards below or next to the **pesticides** card.
5. Connect a piece of yarn from the **pesticides** card to each of the four items to illustrate that they get contaminated by pesticide use.
6. Repeat the sentence pattern **I need (to)** _____ to help learners understand what steps must be taken to protect themselves against pesticides.

NOTE

For students who use chemicals other than pesticides, use nouns and verbs suitable for chemical use. Adapt the situations and associated vocabulary to ones suitable for chemical use and model appropriate sentences.

> **I:** "Pesticides and soil. I need protective clothing." (Hold up
> the **pesticides** and **soil** cards. Hold up the **protective
> clothing** card.)
>
> **I:** "I need protective clothing." (Hold up the **protective
> clothing** card. Motion for the group to repeat the
> sentence.)
>
> **G:** "I need protective clothing."
>
> **I:** "Pesticides and water. I need fresh water." (Hold up the
> **pesticides** and **water** cards. Hold up the **fresh water** card.)
>
> **I:** "I need fresh water." (Hold up the **fresh water** card.
> Motion for the group to repeat the sentence.)
>
> **G:** "I need fresh water."

7. Repeat the pattern above, substituting the suggested
information below.

> Pesticides and plants. I need protective clothing.
> Pesticides and work clothes. I need to wash clothes.

8. Have learners repeat each sentence at least three times.
9. Use the noun cards from Lesson A (**soil, water, plants,** and
work clothes) to prompt practice with the sentence patterns.

Correct Sentence Patterns

> (Soil) I need protective clothing.
> (Water) I need fresh water.
> (Plants) I need protective clothing.
> (Work clothes) I need to wash clothes.

10. Assist learners as necessary.

Comprehension Check

1. Collect the target vocabulary cards and reshuffle them.
2. Place all of the cards faceup on a table or other visible surface.
3. Make statements learned in Oral Language Activity 2 and have
the learners point to the corresponding card.
4. Model the activity before asking learners to respond
independently.

> **I:** "I need protective clothing." (Point to the **protective
> clothing** card. Motion for the learners to repeat and
> point to the correct card.)
>
> **G:** "I need protective clothing." (Point to the **protective
> clothing** card.)

5. Repeat with other statements, assisting the learners as needed.

Oral Language Activity 3

Review the Target Vocabulary

1. Hold up each noun card and motion for the learners to identify each term.
2. Include noun cards from Lesson A to help ensure learners' comprehension.

> **I:** "What's this?" (Hold up the **soap** card. Motion for a response.)
>
> **G:** "Soap."
>
> **I:** "Great. What's this?" (Hold up the **pesticides** card. Motion for a response.)
>
> **G:** "Pesticides."

3. Use the method above to review selected verbs from Lessons A and B.

Lesson A Verbs

Eat	Shower	Wash face
Drink	Use toilet	Wash hands

4. Use mime and gestures as necessary to help the group review terms.

NOTE

Pointing to each word while reading is important to do even if the learners are non-readers or nonliterate.

Grouping Activity

1. Make multiple sets of cards to help facilitate this activity.
2. Hold up the **shower** card and place it at the front of the room.

> **I:** "Shower." (Hold up the **shower** card. Motion for the group to repeat the term.)
>
> **G:** "Shower."
>
> **I:** "What do I need?" (Motion to the **water, shampoo, soap,** and **towel** cards. Mime being unsure of what is needed.)
>
> **I:** "Water, shampoo, soap, towel." (Motion for the group to repeat.)
>
> **G:** "Water, shampoo, soap, towel."

3. Place each card under the **shower** card to illustrate the proper group.
4. Continue with other cards to illustrate the various groups that will help ensure safe use of pesticides. Use the lists below. Adjust groupings as necessary to show groups that will ensure safe use of chemicals.

Groups to Illustrate Safe Use

Shower	Eat/Drink	Use Toilet	Pesticides/Chemicals
Fresh water	Wash hands	Wash hands	Protective clothing
Shampoo	Wash face	Fresh water	Warning sign
Soap	Fresh water	Sink	Warning label
Towel	Soap	Soap	
	Sink	Towel	
	Towel		

5. Review each group with the learners, having them repeat each term.
6. Collect all of the cards except the group headings (**shower, use toilet, eat/drink,** and **pesticides/chemicals**).
7. Reshuffle the cards and hold them up one by one.
8. Ask learners to identify the cards verbally and say the correct group for each one.
9. Assist learners as necessary.

Comprehension Check

1. Distribute the Comprehension Check activity sheet to each learner.
2. Display an enlarged copy of the activity sheet at the front of the room.
3. On the enlarged sheet, point to each picture and have learners identify it.
4. Indicate each grouping and prompt learners to name the category (from Oral Language Activity 3).
5. Point to the pictures in the center. Have learners identify each one and tell which grouping it belongs in.
6. Model how to draw a line from a picture in the center to the question mark in the appropriate grouping.
7. Have the learners draw a line from the picture to the correct grouping on their own activity sheets.
8. Assist learners as necessary.

Oral Language Activity 4

MATERIALS

Large vocabulary cards
(from Lessons A & B)

Introduce the Couplets

1. Write the sample couplets (see example below) in a visible location and read them for the group pointing to each word.
2. Practice the couplets, with the instructor as Speaker 1 and learners as Speaker 2.
3. Prompt responses by holding up appropriate noun or verb cards.

> **Speaker 1:** "What do you need?" (Hold up the **fresh water** card.)
> **Speaker 2:** "I need fresh water."
> **Speaker 1:** "What do you need?" (Hold up the **protective clothing** card.)
> **Speaker 2:** "I need protective clothing."
> **Speaker 1:** "What do you need?" (Hold up the **wash clothes** card.)
> **Speaker 2:** "I need to wash clothes."
> **Speaker 1:** "What do you need?" (Hold up the **shower, soap,** and **shampoo** cards.)
> **Speaker 2:** "I need to shower with soap and shampoo."

NOTE

Pointing to each word while reading is important to do even if the learners are non-readers or nonliterate.

4. Point to each word whenever the couplets are repeated in this activity.
5. Repeat all of the couplets at least three times, using the large vocabulary cards to prompt the learners.

Couplet Activity

1. Practice the couplets. Ask the group to respond to the question by prompting them with large vocabulary cards.
2. Repeat, holding up the large vocabulary cards at random to help ensure that the group practices saying what is necessary for working safely with pesticides.

> **I:** "What do you need?" (Hold up the **fresh water** card.)
> **G:** "I need fresh water."
> **I:** "What do you need?" (Hold up the **protective clothing** card.)
> **G:** "I need protective clothing."
> **I:** "What do you need?" (Hold up the **wash clothes** card.)
> **G:** "I need to wash clothes."
> **I:** "What do you need?" (Hold up the **shower, soap,** and **shampoo** cards.)
> **G:** "I need to shower with soap and shampoo."

3. Assist the group as necessary.

Comprehension Check

1. Use all of the vocabulary cards from Lessons A and B.
2. Spread the cards faceup on the table or another visible surface.
3. Call out terms at random and demonstrate that the learners are to pick up the corresponding cards.
4. Ask the learner who picks up the correct card first to repeat the term that was called. Then have the entire group repeat the term.
5. Repeat the comprehension check more than one time to help ensure the group's understanding of all terms.

Reading Activity

MATERIALS

Large vocabulary cards (from Lessons A & B)

Picture/Word Matching activity sheet (one enlarged and one per learner)

Review

1. Shuffle all of the target vocabulary cards.
2. Show each card to the group while pronouncing each word slowly and clearly.
3. Run a finger under each word to help learners begin to recognize the words apart from the pictures.
4. Have the learners repeat the phrases at least three times.

> **I:** "Sink." (Point to the word.)
> **G:** "Sink."
> **I:** "Sink." (Underline the word with a finger. Motion for the group to repeat the word.)
> **G:** "Sink."

NOTE

Separating words from the pictures should be done gradually and after plenty of practice.

5. Continue to review with the cards, using the pattern above.
6. Fold cards in half to show only the words, to help learners become less dependent on the pictures.
7. Move from group to individual practice as learners become more comfortable reading the words without the assistance of the pictures.

Picture/Word Matching Activity

1. Place the large vocabulary cards in visible locations around the room so that learners can see them.
2. Distribute a Picture/Word Matching activity sheet to each learner.
3. Place an enlarged Picture/Word Matching activity sheet in a visible location.
4. Point to each picture on the enlarged activity sheet and have learners identify each one.
5. Show the learners that the words on the activity sheet can be seen on the vocabulary cards located around the room.

6. Have the group read each word on the activity sheet one by one. Use the example to model on the enlarged activity sheet how to draw a line from each word to a corresponding picture.
7. Encourage learners to use the vocabulary cards around the room to match words and pictures.
8. Have learners complete their own activity sheets.

Writing Activity

Review

1. Shuffle all of the target vocabulary cards.
2. Show each card to the group while pronouncing each word slowly and clearly.
3. Run a finger under each word to help learners begin to recognize the words apart from the pictures.
4. Have the learners repeat the phrases at least three times.

> **I:** "Fresh water." (Point to the words.)
> **G:** "Fresh water."
> **I:** "Fresh water." (Underline the words with a finger. Motion for the group to repeat the words.)
> **G:** "Fresh water."

5. Continue to review with the cards, using the pattern above.
6. Fold cards in half to show only the words, to help learners become less dependent on the pictures.
7. Move from group to individual practice as learners become more comfortable reading the words without the assistance of the pictures.

Label the Pictures Activity

1. Place the large vocabulary cards around the room for learners' reference.
2. Distribute a Label the Pictures activity sheet to each learner.
3. Place an enlarged copy of the activity sheet in a visible location.
4. Point to each picture on the enlarged activity sheet and have learners identify each one.
5. Show the learners that the words on the check sheet can be seen on the vocabulary cards located around the room.
6. Point to the words at the top of the enlarged activity sheet and prompt learners to read each one. If necessary, read the word or phrase aloud while pointing to it and have learners repeat it.

MATERIALS

Large vocabulary cards (from Lessons A & B)

Label the Pictures activity sheet (one enlarged and one per learner)

NOTE

Separating words from the pictures should be done gradually and after plenty of practice.

7. Model for learners how to write the correct word or phrase for each picture on the line next to it. Point to a picture, have learners say the word, demonstrate how to find the correct word in the group at the top of the sheet, and model writing it on the correct line.
8. Have the group label each picture on the lines provided.
9. Assist learners as necessary.

Unit Review Activity

MATERIALS

Unit Review activity sheet (one enlarged and one per learner)

Large vocabulary cards (from Lessons A & B)

NOTE

The Unit Review Activity can be done as a group activity for reinforcing the concepts learned in the lesson or done as an individual activity for assessment purposes.

Safe or Not Safe Review Activity

1. Use large vocabulary cards from Lessons A and B to review the vocabulary and concepts of the unit.
2. Post an enlarged copy of the activity sheet in the front of the room or in another visible location.
3. Point to each picture on the enlarged activity sheet and ask learners to identify it. Make sure learners understand the symbol for No (circle with slash) to indicate that what is pictured is not done or used.
4. Distribute a copy of the Unit Review activity sheet to each learner.
5. On the enlarged activity sheet, point to the picture(s) in each item. Elicit from learners whether the picture or combination of pictures shown in the item is safe or not. Model for learners how to check OK if the item indicates safe behavior or conditions and Not OK if the behavior or conditions are not safe.
6. If appropriate, add or substitute pictures and use realia to review safe behavior and conditions for working with other chemicals.
7. Ask learners to complete the activity on their own sheets. If necessary, use the enlarged activity sheet to model for learners how to check the correct column to indicate that the item is OK or Not OK.

DANGER PELIGRO
PESTICIDES PESTICIDAS

KEEP OUT
NO ENTRE

Unit 2 *Handling Dangerous Chemicals* Lesson A *Life Skill*

Pesticides

✂ -

Plants

Before

Unit 2 *Handling Dangerous Chemicals* Lesson A

After

Unit 2 *Handling Dangerous Chemicals* Lesson A

✂

WARNING

WARNING

Chemicals

Unit 2 *Handling Dangerous Chemicals* Lesson A

Shampoo

Clean Hair
Extra Body
conditioning
Shampoo
21.75FL OZ (643mL)

✂

Soap

2 white bars
Clean Skin
light moisturizers for normal skin
135g (4.75 each TOTAL NET WT 270g (9.5oz) 2 moisturizing bars

Water

Unit 2 *Handling Dangerous Chemicals Lesson A*

Soil

Unit 2 *Handling Dangerous Chemicals Lesson A*

Work clothes

Eat

Shower

Unit 2 *Handling Dangerous Chemicals* Lesson A

Drink

Large Vocabulary Cards

Unit 2 *Handling Dangerous Chemicals* Lesson A

Use toilet

✂ -

Wash face

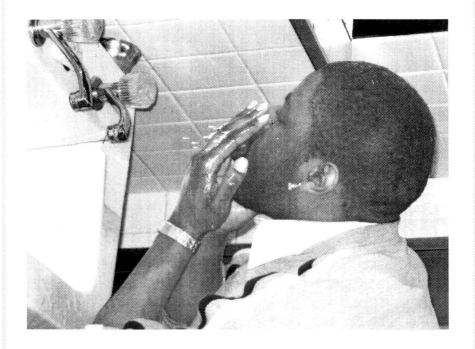

Yes

No

Wash hands

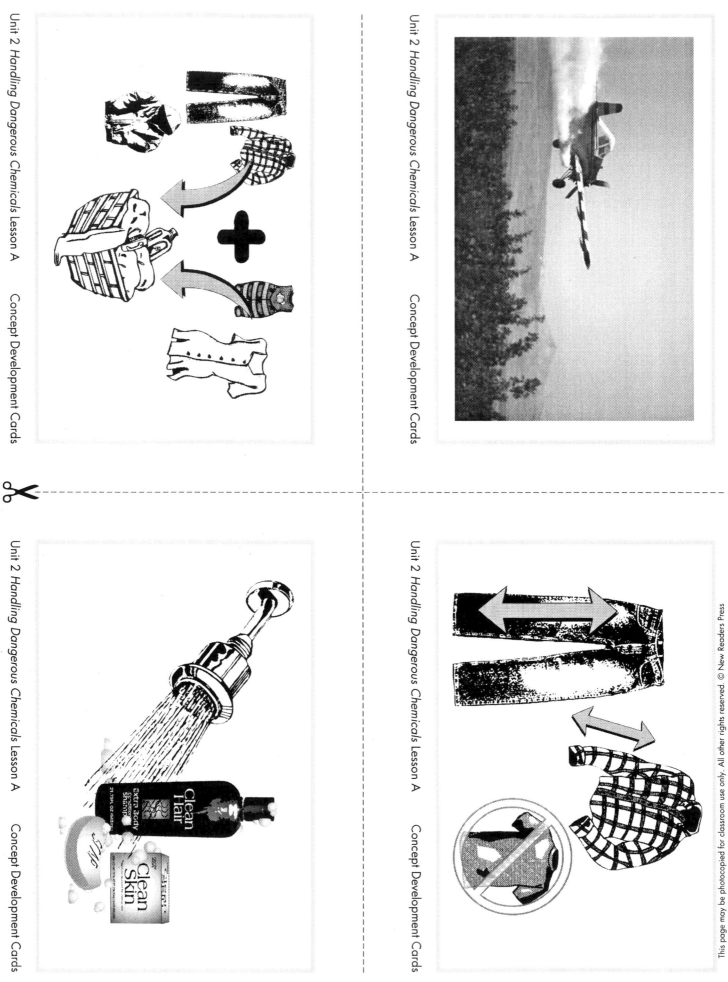

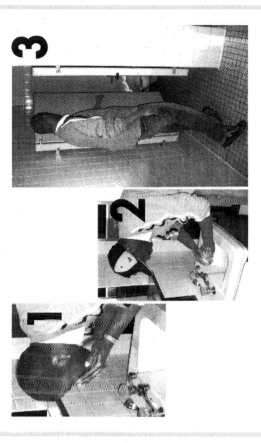

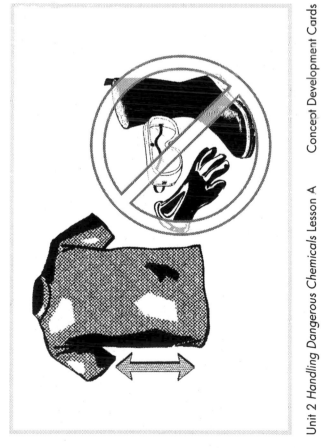

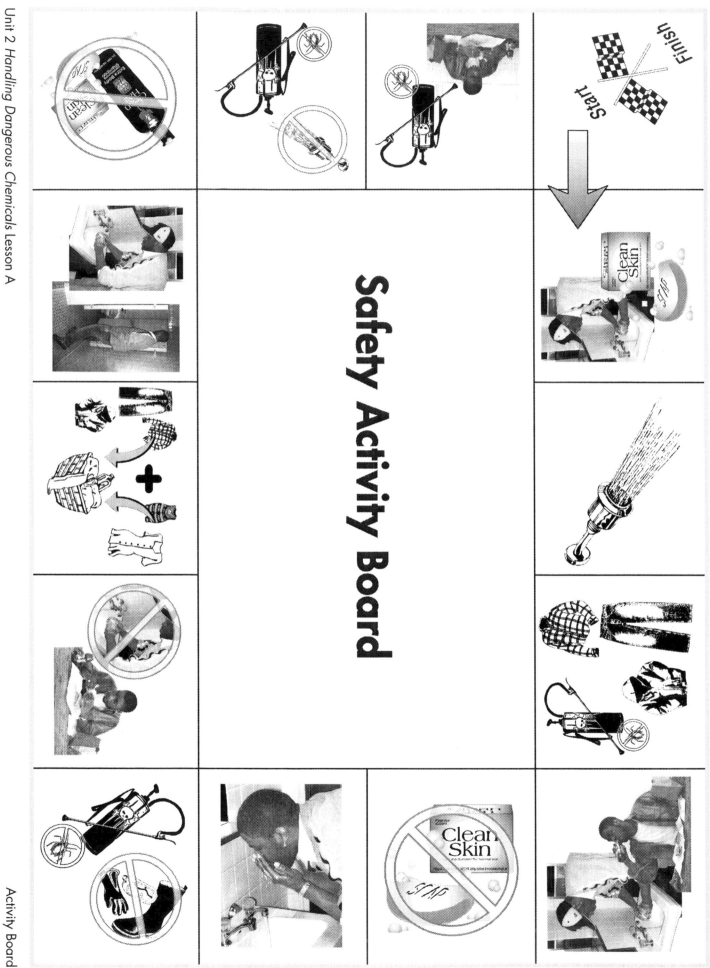

Safety Activity Board

Die Pattern and Word Strips

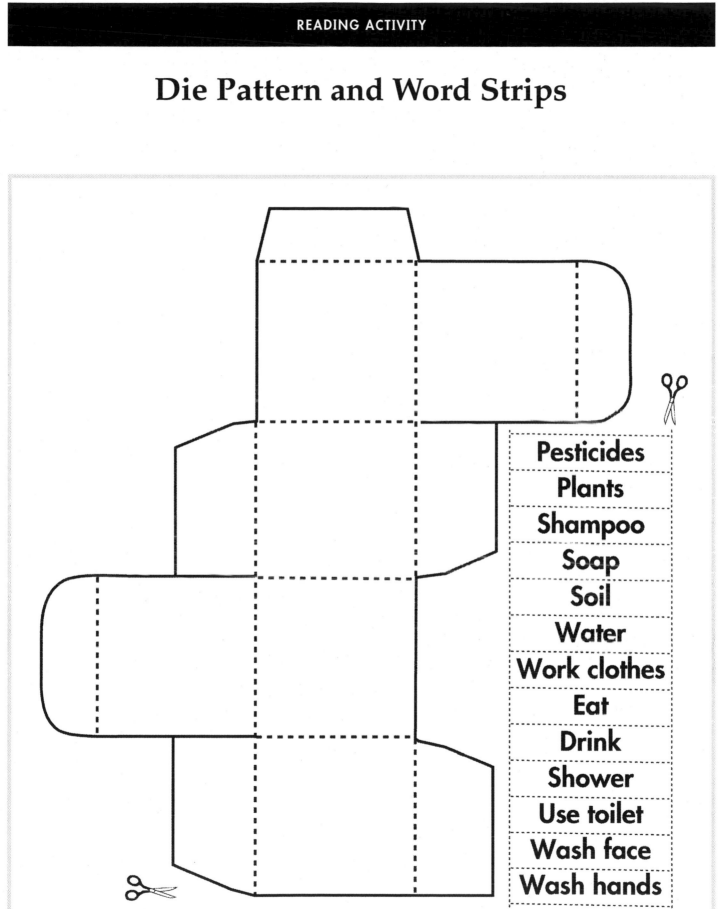

Pesticides
Plants
Shampoo
Soap
Soil
Water
Work clothes
Eat
Drink
Shower
Use toilet
Wash face
Wash hands

Unit 2 *Handling Dangerous Chemicals* Lesson A *Life Skill*

Reading Activity Sheet

Sentence Completion

Look at the pictures. Write the missing words. Complete the sentences.

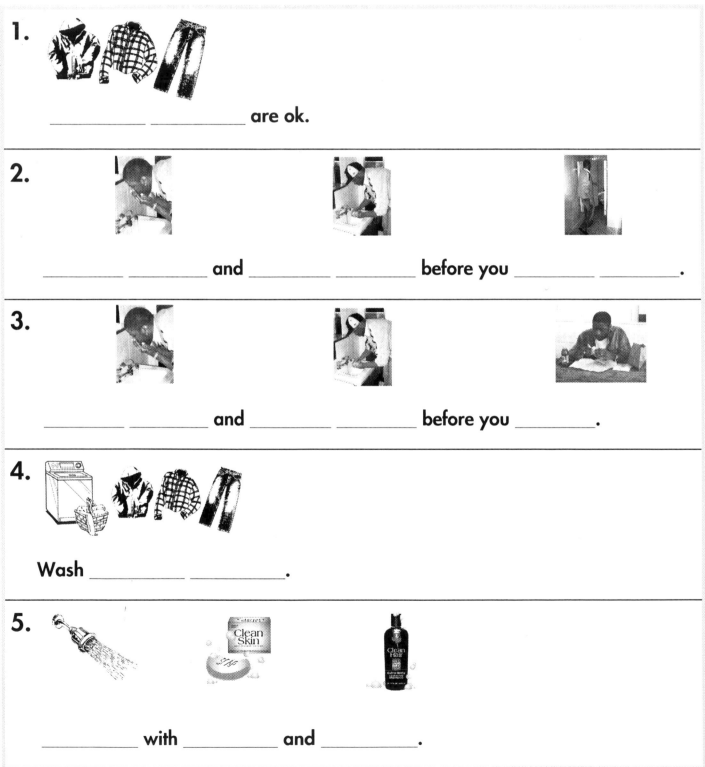

1. _____ _____ are ok.

2. _____ _____ and _____ _____ before you _____ _____ .

3. _____ _____ and _____ _____ before you _____ .

4. Wash _____ _____ .

5. _____ with _____ and _____ .

Unit 2 *Handling Dangerous Chemicals* Lesson A *Life Skill*   Writing Activity Sheet

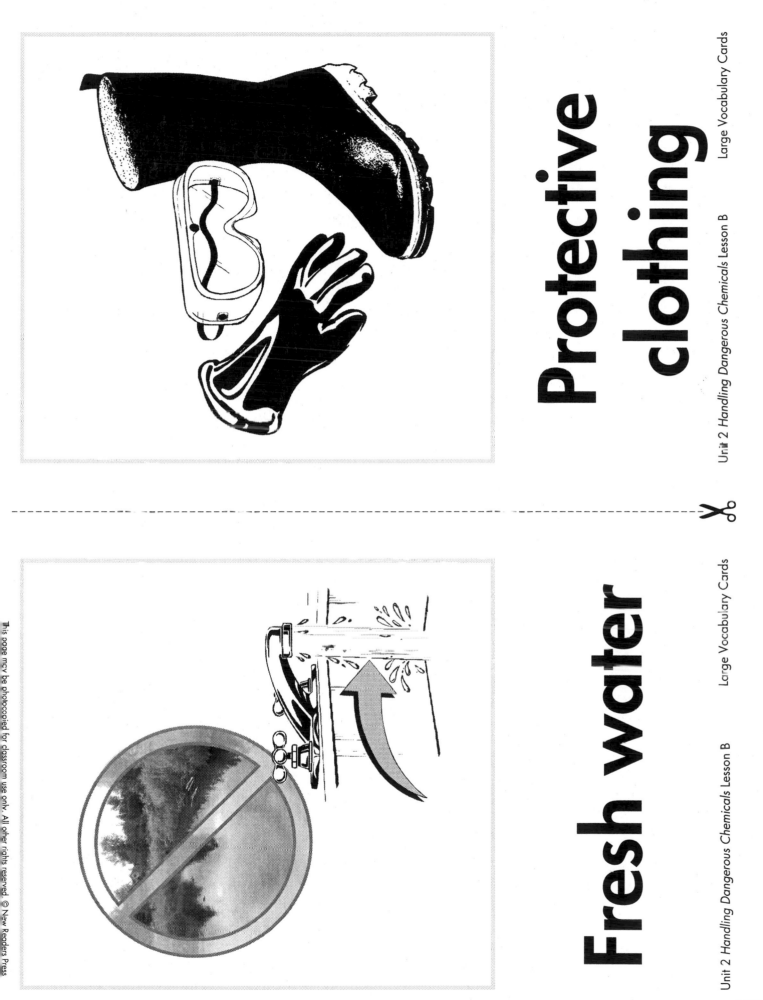

Protective clothing

Unit 2 *Handling Dangerous Chemicals* Lesson B

Fresh water

Large Vocabulary Cards

Unit 2 *Handling Dangerous Chemicals* Lesson B

Sink

✂ -

Toilet

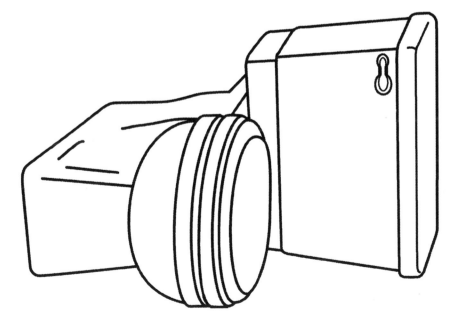

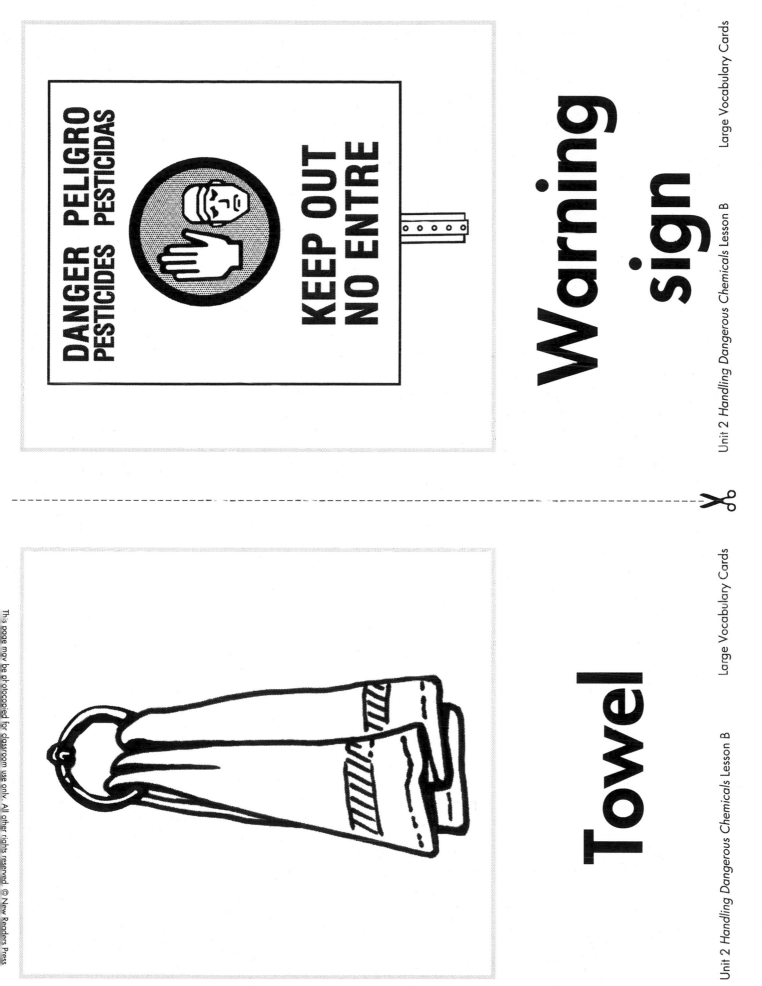

Warning sign

Large Vocabulary Cards

Towel

Large Vocabulary Cards

Warning label

Comprehension Check Activity

One picture is missing from each group. Draw a line from each picture
in the center to the group where it belongs.

Unit 2 *Handling Dangerous Chemicals* Lesson B *Civic Responsibility*

Activity Sheet

Picture/Word Matching Activity

Draw a line from each picture to the correct word.

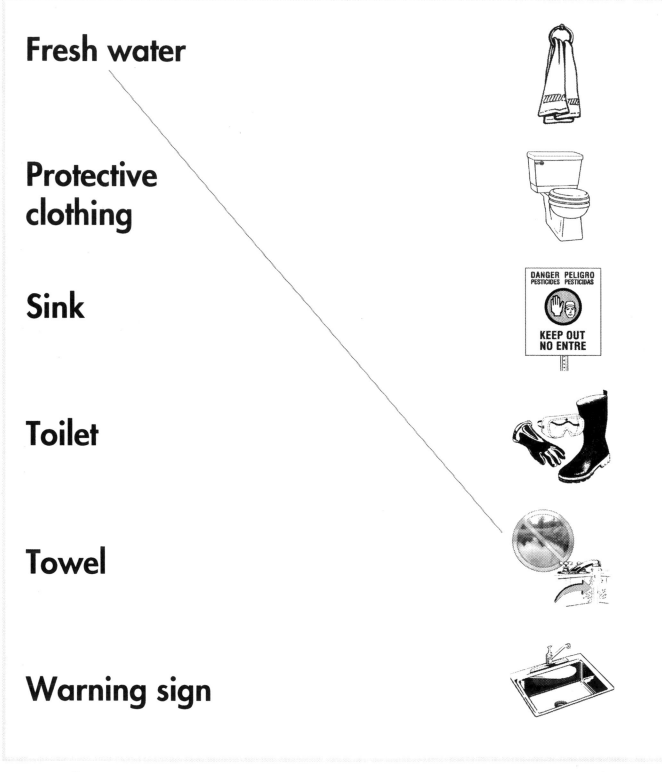

Fresh water

Protective clothing

Sink

Toilet

Towel

Warning sign

Label the Pictures Activity

Look at the pictures. Write the words on the lines.

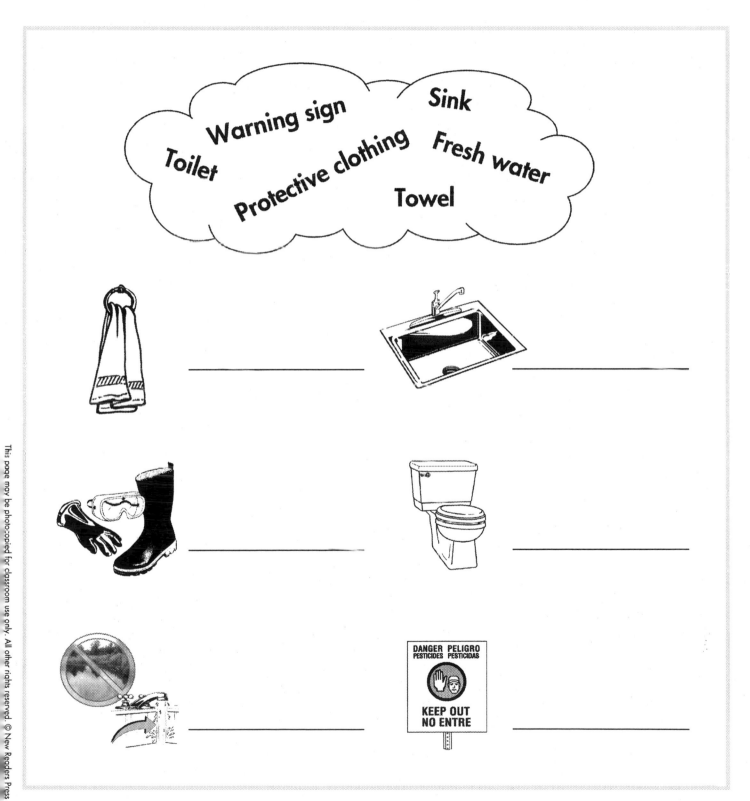

Warning sign   Sink

Toilet   Protective clothing   Fresh water

Towel

DANGER PELIGRO
PESTICIDES PESTICIDAS

KEEP OUT
NO ENTRE

Unit 2 *Handling Dangerous Chemicals* Lesson B *Civic Responsibility*

Writing Activity Sheet

Look at the pictures. Check OK for safe behaviors. Check Not OK for unsafe behaviors.

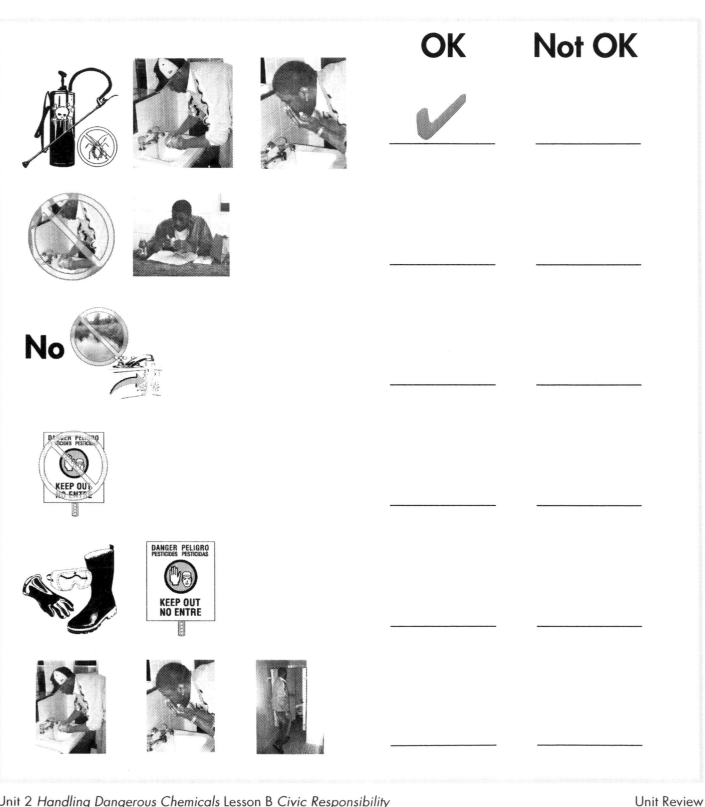

	OK	Not OK
	✔	

Unit 3

Medicine and Controlled Substances

Getting and Taking Medicine

VOCABULARY

NOUNS
Directions
Doctor
Drugstore
Medicine
Pharmacy
Prescription
Supermarket

ADJECTIVES
Over-the-counter
Prescription

VERB PHRASES
Ask for help
Follow directions
Written by doctor

Objective

To help learners understand the difference between over-the-counter and prescription medications and the appropriate uses of each

Materials Included

- Central theme picture
- Large reproducible vocabulary cards
- Picture Bingo boards
- Small **doctor** cards
- Word Search activity sheet
- Fill in the Missing Words activity sheet
- **Yes/No** cards

Materials Needed

- Additional instructor copy (enlarged) of the activity sheets
- Medicine bottles and packages (empty but with labels)
- Pharmacy circulars
- Pictures of medicine and medicine packages, drugstores, pharmacies, and supermarkets (e.g., from magazines, newspapers, and advertising circulars)
- Yarn or string
- Pens or pencils and paper
- Bingo board markers (paper clips, buttons, dried beans, coins, or other small objects)
- Instructor-made **question mark** cards

Central Theme Picture

MATERIALS

Theme picture

POSSIBLE RESPONSES

Bottle

Buy

Man

Medicine

Pharmacy

Sick

Store

Woman

Introduce the Theme Picture

1. Show learners the theme picture and ask for a response.
2. Encourage learners to say anything about the picture that they can.

> **I:** "What's happening in this picture?" (Point out key things about the picture to elicit a response.)

Oral Language Activity 1

MATERIALS

Large noun cards

Medicine bottles and packages

Pictures of medicine and medicine packages, drugstores, pharmacies, and supermarkets

Pharmacy circulars

Bingo board markers (paper clips, buttons, dried beans, coins, or other small objects)

NOTE

The target word **prescription** is taught first as a noun, referring to the paper written by a doctor and taken by a patient to a pharmacy. Then it is used as an adjective in the phrase *prescription medicine*, as distinguished from *over-the-counter medicine*.

Introduce the Target Nouns

1. Show each large noun card to the group while pronouncing each word slowly and clearly.

> **I:** "Medicine." (Hold up the **medicine** card. Show pictures of medicine and/or real medicine bottles and packages. Motion for the learners to repeat the word.)
>
> **G:** "Medicine."
>
> **I:** "Good. Medicine." (Motion for learners to repeat together.)
>
> **G:** "Medicine."
>
> **I:** "Very good. What's this?" (Hold up the **medicine** card. Motion for a response.)
>
> **G:** "Medicine."

2. Show the vocabulary cards for each target noun and ask the group to repeat each term.
3. Use pictures of drugstores, pharmacies, and supermarkets to reinforce meanings.
4. Use medicine bottles and packages to associate the word *directions* with the location of where to look for directions on real medicine labels.
5. Have the group repeat the new terms at least three times.

Picture Bingo Activity

1. Distribute one Bingo board to each learner.
2. Give each learner a set of small Bingo board markers.

3. Show learners how they can win with five pictures in a row (horizontally, vertically, or diagonally).
4. Use the large noun cards to prompt learners. Shuffle the large noun cards and place them in a basket, box, or envelope.
5. Ask learners to verbally identify the vocabulary item each time a card is chosen.
6. Model the game for learners. Draw a card. Show the card to the group and elicit a response or, if necessary, identify the card verbally for learners.
7. Have learners mark their boards on the square corresponding to the noun card drawn, using one of their Bingo board markers. Ask them to repeat each word as they mark their boards.

> **I:** "What's this?" (Hold up the **medicine** card and motion for a response.)
> **G:** "Medicine."
> **I:** "Great. Medicine." (Show learners how to find **medicine** on the board and how to mark it. Motion for them to repeat the word.)
> **G:** "Medicine."

8. Have a learner draw a card and hold it up. Ask the group to identify the vocabulary term pictured.
9. Continue the game by asking each learner to draw a card and have the entire group say each vocabulary word drawn. If necessary, prompt learners by saying the word and having the group repeat.
10. Continue the activity until a learner has five pictures in a row marked (horizontally, vertically, or diagonally) and have that learner call out *Bingo.*
11. Once a learner has gotten Bingo, rotate the Bingo boards, reshuffle the cards, and do the activity again for additional practice.

NOTE

For Bingo, a learner has to have five pictures marked horizontally, vertically, or diagonally.

Comprehension Check

1. Collect the target noun cards and reshuffle them.
2. Hold up the cards one by one, identifying the words correctly and incorrectly at random.
3. Model how to say Yes when the card is correctly identified, and No when it is incorrectly identified.

> **I:** "Supermarket." (Hold up the **supermarket** card.)
>
> **I:** "Supermarket. Yes." (Point to the **supermarket** card and nod in agreement. Motion for the learners to repeat.)
>
> **G:** "Yes."
>
> **I:** "Medicine." (Hold up the **supermarket** card again.)
>
> **I:** "Medicine. No." (Point to the **supermarket** card and motion for disagreement. Ask the learners to repeat.)
>
> **G:** "No."

4. Repeat words as necessary to ensure learners' understanding.

Oral Language Activity 2

Introduce the Verb Phrases

MATERIALS

Medicine bottles and packages

Large **doctor, pharmacy,** and **prescription** cards

Small **doctor** cards

Theme picture

Instructor-made **question mark** cards

Pens or pencils and paper (for each learner)

1. Introduce each verb phrase, using realia or mime, pronouncing each phrase slowly and clearly.

> **I:** "Follow directions." (Hold up a bottle of medicine and point to the directions. Mime reading the label while nodding your head to indicate Yes. Mime taking the medicine as directed. Motion for the group to repeat.)
>
> **G:** "Follow directions."
>
> **I:** "Good. Follow directions." (Motion for learners to repeat.)
>
> **G:** "Follow directions."
>
> **I:** "Very good. Follow directions." (Hold up a medicine bottle and mime following the directions. Motion for learners to repeat.)
>
> **G:** "Follow directions."

2. If appropriate, repeat the format for **follow directions** using a medicine package, to show learners where to find directions on the box.

3. Continue introducing the verb phrases **(ask for help, written by doctor),** using mime and realia as suggested on the following page.

4. Have the group repeat the new phrases at least three times.

Suggestions

Follow directions—use a medicine bottle or package to demonstrate following directions, as described previously

Ask for help—look at a medicine bottle or package and hold up a **question mark** card or write question marks on the board or on chart paper; use the **doctor** card to mime asking the doctor for help and use the theme picture or **pharmacy** card to mime asking the pharmacist for help

Written by doctor—use the **doctor, pharmacy,** and **prescription** cards; associate the doctor with writing a paper (a prescription) that is given to the pharmacy, followed by receipt of medication, indicated by using a medicine bottle

Verb Phrase TPR (Total Physical Response)

1. Distribute realia and other materials (medicine bottles, instructor-provided **question mark** cards, small **doctor** cards, paper, and pens or pencils) so that each learner has a set of necessary TPR props.
2. Motion for the learners to listen carefully by holding one hand up to an ear with palm open.
3. Call out a verb phrase and associate it with an action and realia (as suggested above).
4. Have the group repeat each verb phrase with its accompanying action, mime, and/or realia.
5. Have the group repeat the actions and say the verb phrases at least three times.
6. Move from calling out target verb phrases while showing learners the accompanying action, mime and/or realia to calling out the target verb phrases as the only prompt.
7. Have learners mime and/or show the appropriate realia and actions for each verb phrase.
8. Repeat any phrases the group has difficulty remembering.

Comprehension Check

1. Collect all of the realia and place it on a table or on another available surface.
2. Call out each target verb phrase and motion for the learners to try to pick up the corresponding realia and mime each verb phrase.
3. Have the learner who picks up the appropriate realia first mime the verb phrase using the item.
4. Have learners repeat each verb phrase as it is mimed.
5. Move on to Oral Language Activity 3 when the group has a solid comprehension of the target verb phrases.

Oral Language Activity 3

MATERIALS

Large vocabulary cards

Medicine bottles and packages

Small **doctor** cards (used for labeling prescription medication bottles)

Yarn, string, or other method for making circles

Yes/No cards (one set per learner)

Introduce the Adjectives

1. Prepare a set of medicine bottles to indicate prescription medicines by attaching a small **doctor** card to each. Keep a set of medicine bottles and/or packages with no **doctor** card attached to use as over-the-counter medications.
2. Show each large adjective card to the group while pronouncing each word slowly and clearly.

> **I:** "Over-the-counter." (Hold up the **over-the-counter** card. Motion for the group to repeat.)
>
> **G:** "Over-the-counter."
>
> **I:** "Good. Over-the-counter." (Hold up a medicine bottle and or package that could be bought over the counter. Motion for learners to repeat.)
>
> **G:** "Over-the-counter."
>
> **I:** "Very good. Over-the-counter." (Hold up the **over-the-counter** card. Motion for the group to repeat.)
>
> **G:** "Over-the-counter."
>
> **I:** "Over-the-counter medicine." (Hold up the **over-the-counter** and **medicine** cards together. Motion for the group to repeat.)
>
> **G:** "Over-the-counter medicine."

3. Present the other target adjective (**prescription**) and the phrase **prescription medicine,** using the format above.
4. Show medicine bottles with small **doctor** cards attached to indicate prescription medications.
5. Have the group repeat each new term and phrase at least three times.
6. Review the vocabulary from Oral Language Activity 1 and Oral Language Activity 2 by showing cards or miming with realia and motioning for a response.
7. Assist learners as needed.

Prescription or Over-the-Counter Sorting Activity

1. Use the medicine bottles with small **doctor** cards attached, prepared above, to indicate prescription medications in this activity.
2. Make two large circles with yarn or string. Place the large **prescription** card in one circle and the **over-the-counter** card in the other circle.
3. Have the learners identify the category of each circle by identifying each card verbally.

4. Distribute a variety of medications to the group, some with a small **doctor** card attached and others without the card. Make sure that the items used for over-the-counter medications are in packages similar to those bought over the counter, not in bottles with prescription labels.
5. Show the group that medications labeled with the **doctor** card belong in the **prescription** circle and the other medications belong in the **over-the-counter** circle. Make sure learners associate the doctor with prescription medicine.
6. Have learners verbally identify each bottle or package as prescription medicine or over-the-counter medicine as they put it in the appropriate circle.
7. Redistribute the medications to the group to sort again, for more verbal practice.
8. Assist learners as necessary.

Comprehension Check

1. Distribute **Yes/No** cards to each learner.
2. Hold up medicine bottles one by one and identify them correctly and incorrectly at random as over-the-counter medicine or prescription medicine.
3. Ask the group to hold up the **Yes** card if the medicine is correctly identified and the **No** card if the medicine is incorrectly identified.

> **I:** "Over-the-counter." (Hold up a medicine bottle without a **doctor** card. Motion for a response.)
> **G:** "Yes." (Hold up the **Yes** card.)

4. Continue identifying other bottles of medicine correctly or incorrectly at random to check learners' comprehension of the concepts of **over-the-counter** and **prescription medicine.**

Oral Language Activity 4

MATERIALS

Large vocabulary cards

Realia, including medicine bottles, magazine pictures, pharmacy circulars

An instructor-made **question mark** card

Introduce the Dialogue

1. Write the model dialogue (see example on next page) on the board or other visible surface.
2. Introduce the dialogue, pointing to each line as it is presented and holding up the corresponding cards.

NOTE

It may be useful to help learners understand that **pharmacy** can refer to both a type of store, one which sells over-the-counter drugs as well as prescription medicine (and other things), and to a place within a store where prescription medicine is sold. They should understand that they can find a pharmacy to sell prescription medicine in some supermarkets as well as in stores called pharmacies or drugstores.

Speaker 1:	"Where do you go for over-the-counter medicine?" (Hold up the **over-the-counter, supermarket,** and **drugstore** cards. Motion for the group to respond.)
Speaker 2:	"Drugstore or supermarket."
Speaker 1:	"Where do you get a prescription?" (Hold up the **doctor** and **prescription** cards.)
Speaker 2:	"Doctor."
Speaker 1:	"Where do you go for prescription medicine?" (Hold up the **prescription** and **pharmacy** cards.)
Speaker 2:	"Pharmacy."
Speaker 1:	"What should you do?" (Hold up several bottles of medicine and a **question mark** card. Motion for the group to respond.)
Speaker 2:	"Ask for help."
Speaker 1:	"What should you do?" (Hold up a medicine bottle or package and point to the directions. Hold up the **directions** card to represent *follow directions.* Motion for the group to respond.)
Speaker 2:	"Follow directions."

3. Use vocabulary cards, mime, and gestures as appropriate to prompt the group.
4. Perform the dialogue as Speaker 1 and have the group respond as Speaker 2.

Dialogue Activity

1. Write the sample dialogue (see example on the following page) on the board or on chart paper and read it for the group, pointing to each word.
2. Perform the dialogue as a group, using the written example, with cards and realia to accompany each step.
3. Practice the dialogue with the instructor as Speaker 1 and the group as Speaker 2.

Speaker 1:	"Where do you go for over-the-counter medicine?" (Hold up the **over-the-counter, supermarket,** and **drugstore** cards. Motion for the group to respond.)
Speaker 2:	"Drugstore or supermarket."
Speaker 1:	"Where do you get a prescription?" (Hold up the **doctor** and **prescription** cards.)
Speaker 2:	"Doctor."
Speaker 1:	"Where do you go for prescription medicine?" (Hold up the **prescription** and **pharmacy** cards.)
Speaker 2:	"Pharmacy."
Speaker 1:	"What should you do?" (Hold up several bottles of medicine and an instructor-made **question mark** card. Motion for the group to respond.)
Speaker 2:	"Ask for help."
Speaker 1:	"What should you do?" (Hold up a medicine bottle and point to the directions. Hold up the **directions** card to represent **follow directions.** Motion for the group to respond.)
Speaker 2:	"Follow directions."

4. Point to each word whenever the dialogue is repeated in this activity.
5. Use vocabulary cards, realia, gestures, and mime as necessary to prompt the dialogue practice.
6. Assist learners as necessary.

Comprehension Check

1. Hold up two vocabulary cards and identify one correctly.
2. Ask the group to point to the card that was correctly identified, as in the example below.

I:	"Directions." (Hold up the **directions** and **pharmacy** cards. Motion for learners to repeat and point to the correct card.)
G:	"Directions." (Point to the **directions** card.)

3. Continue with other pairs to ensure the learner's comprehension of all the vocabulary.

Reading Activity

MATERIALS

Large vocabulary cards

Word Search activity sheet (one enlarged and one per learner)

Review

1. Shuffle all of the target vocabulary cards.
2. Show each card to the group while pronouncing each word slowly and clearly.

3. Run a finger under each word to help learners begin to recognize the words apart from the pictures.

4. Have the learners repeat the terms at least three times.

> **I:** "Supermarket." (Point to the word.)
>
> **G:** "Supermarket."
>
> **I:** "Supermarket." (Underline the word with a finger. Motion for the group to repeat the word.)
>
> **G:** "Supermarket."

NOTE

Separating words from pictures should be done gradually and after plenty of practice.

5. Continue to review with the cards, using the pattern above.

6. Fold cards in half to show only the words, to help learners become less dependent on the pictures.

7. Move from group to individual practice as learners become more comfortable reading the words without the assistance of the pictures.

Word Search Activity

1. Pass out a Word Search activity sheet to each learner.

2. Put the enlarged copy of the activity sheet in the front of the room or in another visible location.

3. Point to each picture at the top of the enlarged activity sheet and ask learners to identify the picture verbally. Run a finger under the word next to the picture and motion for learners to read the word.

4. Using the enlarged activity sheet, show the learners how to use the pictures and words listed at the top to locate words in the word search grid.

5. Choose a word from the list to locate in the word search grid.

6. Read the word for the learners and point to the picture that represents it.

7. Demonstrate how to look in the word search grid for the word written under the picture.

8. Model finding the word, pointing to each letter in the word. Then demonstrate on the enlarged sheet how to circle the word that is found.

9. Have the learners say each word from the list before they begin their search. Have them complete their own Word Search activity sheets.

10. Assist learners as necessary.

11. When learners have completed their activity sheets, have volunteers come up and circle the rest of the words on the enlarged activity sheet.

12. Check learners' reading by pointing to a circled word on the enlarged activity sheet and having learners read the word.

Writing Activity

MATERIALS

Large vocabulary cards

Fill in the Missing Words activity sheet (one enlarged and one per learner)

Review

1. Shuffle all of the target vocabulary cards.
2. Show each card to the group while pronouncing each word slowly and clearly.
3. Run a finger under each word to help learners begin to recognize the words apart from the pictures.
4. Have the learners repeat the vocabulary at least three times.

> **I:** "Medicine." (Point to the word.)
> **G:** "Medicine."
> **I:** "Medicine." (Underline the word with a finger. Motion for the group to repeat the word.)
> **G:** "Medicine."

5. Continue to review with the cards, using the pattern above.
6. Fold cards in half to show only the words, to help learners become less dependent on the pictures.
7. Move from group to individual practice as learners become more comfortable reading the words without the assistance of the pictures.

NOTE

Separating words from pictures should be done gradually and after plenty of practice.

Fill in the Missing Words Activity

1. Place the large noun and adjective cards on the table or in another visible location.
2. Have the learners use the vocabulary cards to assist with the Fill in the Missing Words activity sheet.
3. Place an enlarged Fill in the Missing Words activity sheet on the board or in another visible location.
4. Distribute an activity sheet to each learner.
5. Ask the learners to identify the missing words verbally and write them in the spaces provided.
6. Show the learners how to use the large vocabulary cards for assistance.
7. Complete the activity sheet as a group.

Lesson B - Civic Responsibility

Illegal Drugs

VOCABULARY

NOUNS
Cocaine

Crack

Ecstasy

Illegal drugs

LSD

Marijuana

User

VERBS
Arrest

Buy

Leave

Possess

Sell

Use

ADJECTIVE
Illegal

SENTENCES
It's Not OK to possess drugs.

It's Not OK to use drugs.

Drug users are Not OK.

Say NO to illegal drugs.

Objectives

- To ensure that learners understand that possession of, association with, and/or use of certain drugs is illegal
- To help learners understand the consequences of possession, association with, and/or use of illegal drugs
- To teach learners methods of refusing these illegal drugs

Materials Included

- Large reproducible vocabulary cards
- Find the Correct Word activity sheet
- Drug Information activity sheet
- **OK/Not OK** cards (page 208)

Materials Needed

- Real or play money
- Real or instructor-made replicas of price tags
- A pen or a pencil
- A cooking tool or small household tool (e.g., a hammer)
- Pictures of medicines (prescription and over-the-counter) and illegal drugs
- Medicine bottles and packages (from Lesson A)
- Magazine or newspaper pictures of people being arrested, a police officer, a person doing something illegal (e.g., stealing), people buying and selling products, people walking away from a group, car, house, etc.
- Pictures of commercial products and of a house or car
- Additional instructor copy (enlarged) of the activity sheets

Civics Introduction

Illegal Drugs

In the U.S., illegal drugs are available for purchase in urban, suburban, and rural settings. Being a drug user has serious health and legal risks. Using drugs, even occasionally, can alter moods, damage or dissolve relationships, interfere with job performance, and even result in financial ruin. In addition to the physical and emotional consequences of dependence on drugs, using, possessing, producing, or selling illegal drugs is against the law.

In response to the growth in illegal drug use and a growing number of drug-related arrests, a movement that came to be known as the War on Drugs began in the 1970s. The focus was not only on stronger legal response to illegal drug sale and use, but also on particular educational efforts and persuasive advertising to heighten awareness of the health risks and legal consequences associated with using and possessing illegal drugs. The intent was to reduce the number of drug arrests and incarcerations as well as the number of deaths and serious health problems caused by illegal drugs.

This topic is important for newly arrived, non-English-speaking adults because punishment in the U.S. for use, possession, production, and sale of illegal drugs may differ from that in their native countries. New arrivals need to be aware of the consequences for involvement with illegal drugs in the U.S. They need to understand that for immigrants, those consequences may include deportation and may block any chance of future citizenship. This lesson combines the consequences for sale, possession, and/or use of illegal drugs with the importance of not associating with users and of avoiding illegal drugs overall.

Oral Language Activity 1

MATERIALS

Large noun cards

Pictures of medicines (prescription and over-the-counter) and illegal drugs

Medicine bottles and packages (from Lesson A)

Yes/No cards (one set per learner)

OK/Not OK cards

NOTE

It may be appropriate to teach learners the names of other illegal drugs that they need to avoid, e.g., heroin or meth, depending on what is common in their area.

Introduce the Target Nouns and Adjective

1. Show each large noun card to the group while pronouncing each word slowly and clearly.

> **I:** "Illegal drugs." (Hold up the **illegal drugs** card. Motion for the group to repeat together.)
> **G:** "Illegal drugs."
> **I:** "Good. Illegal drugs." (Motion for the group to repeat.)
> **G:** "Illegal drugs."
> **I:** "Illegal drugs." (Motion for the group to repeat. Put the **illegal drugs** card at the front of the room.)
> **G:** "Illegal drugs."

2. Introduce the term **illegal** by placing the **illegal** card at the front of the room with the **illegal drugs** card.
3. Convey the meaning of **illegal** with the frowning police officer and image of jail on the **illegal** card.
4. Teach **ecstasy, cocaine/crack, LSD,** and **marijuana** using the method above.
5. Place each card with a drug name under the **illegal drugs** and **illegal** cards at the front of the room so that the group understands that each substance is an illegal drug.
6. Introduce the concept of **user** by associating the person on the **user** card with each of the illegal drugs shown on the cards (including the general **illegal drugs** card).
7. Say each word and have the group repeat each one three times.
8. Repeat any words more than three times as necessary (with the group, with pairs, or individually).

Sorting Activity

1. Place the **OK** and **Not OK** cards on the board or on another visible surface.
2. Put the **illegal** card with the **Not OK** card.
3. Hold up each vocabulary card and ask the group to decide if it is a legal (OK) or illegal (Not OK) drug.
4. Use vocabulary from Lesson A as well as medicine bottles and pictures of medicine (prescription and over-the-counter) and illegal drugs, to ensure adequate practice of the concept.

> **I:** "What's this?" (Hold up the **medicine** card. Motion for a response.)
>
> **G:** "Medicine."
>
> **I:** "OK or Not OK?" (Motion for a response.)
>
> **G:** "OK."
>
> **I:** "What's this?" (Hold up the **marijuana** card. Motion for a response.)
>
> **G:** "Marijuana."
>
> **I:** "OK or Not OK?" (Motion for a response.)
>
> **G:** "Not OK."
>
> **I:** "Not OK and . . . ?" (Point to the **illegal** card. Motion for a response.)
>
> **G:** "Illegal."

4. Continue to have the learners decide in which group the cards, magazine pictures, or medicine bottles should be placed.
5. Have learners respond to cards or pictures of illegal drugs by saying both *Not OK* and *illegal.*
6. Reshuffle and distribute cards and realia to learners at random (if possible, at least one card or item per learner). Have individual learners place the cards, pictures, and realia in the correct groups.
7. Ask each learner to identify the card, picture, or item that he or she is placing and the appropriate group (**OK** or **Not OK/Illegal**) into which it is being placed.
8. Assist learners as necessary.

Comprehension Check

1. Hold up cards, realia, or magazine pictures and tell the group if the drug is OK or Not OK (illegal). Identify drugs correctly or incorrectly at random.
2. Ask learners to say if the identification is correct (Yes) or incorrect (No).
3. Model the learners' responses before asking them to respond independently.

> **I:** "OK." (Hold up the **medicine** card.)
>
> **I:** "OK. Yes." (Hold up the **medicine** card. Motion for learners to repeat the response.)
>
> **G:** "OK. Yes."
>
> **I:** "OK." (Hold up the **LSD** card.)
>
> **I:** "OK. No." (Hold up the **LSD** card. Hold up the **illegal** card. Motion for learners to repeat the response.)
>
> **G:** "No."
>
> **I:** "Not OK." (Hold up the **cocaine/crack** card. Motion for a response.)
>
> **G:** "Not OK. Yes."

4. Continue with the nouns referring to drugs from Lessons A and B to ensure understanding and comprehension of what is OK and Not OK (illegal). Include the **user** card from Lesson B and identify it as Not OK.
5. Assist learners as necessary.

Oral Language Activity 2

MATERIALS

Large verb cards

Large noun cards

Real or play money

Realia and pictures

Yes/No cards

Introduce the Target Verbs

1. Show each large verb card to the group while pronouncing each word slowly and clearly.

> **I:** "Arrest." (Hold up the **arrest** card. Motion for the group to repeat.)
> **G:** "Arrest."
> **I:** "Good. Arrest." (Motion for the group to repeat.)
> **G:** "Arrest."
> **I:** "Arrest." (Motion for the group to repeat. Put the **arrest** card at the front of the room.)
> **G:** "Arrest."

2. Introduce the other verbs (**buy, leave, possess, sell,** and **use**) one by one and place the cards at the front of the room.
3. Use mime, gestures, and realia or pictures to help illustrate the meanings of the verbs.

Suggestions for Introducing Verbs

Arrest—show pictures of people being arrested, of a police officer, and of someone doing something illegal, e.g., stealing

Buy—mime being in a store and show the exchange of money from you to another person for a product; show pictures of people in stores buying and selling things

Leave—stand up and wave good bye to the group, walk away, and go out the door of the room

Possess—show the group **possess** by placing an item in your pocket, purse, book bag, or briefcase or show a picture of a car or house and associate it as yours

Sell—put a price tag on an item or picture of a product and mime the exchange of money from someone else to you for it.

Use—demonstrate using a pencil, pen, cooking tool, or small household tool to accomplish a task.

4. Say each verb and have the group repeat each one three times.
5. Repeat any verb more than three times as necessary (with the group, with pairs, or individually).

6. Use the noun cards (from Lesson B) in conjunction with the verbs gradually and after plenty of practice.
7. Assist learners as necessary.

Acting Out the Verbs Activity

1. Place the verb cards facedown on a table or other available surface for the learners to select from.
2. Place the realia and pictures around the room for learners to use as needed.
3. Model the process of choosing a verb card to act out for the group.
4. Choose a card, look at the picture and word, and act out the word using gestures, mime, and realia.
5. Ask the group to guess which verb is being acted out and identify it verbally.
6. Demonstrate the activity with several other verbs. Have the learners guess which verb is being acted out.
7. Have the learners take turns choosing a card and acting out the verb for the other group members to guess.
8. Ask the group to say each verb together for more verbal practice.
9. Assist learners as necessary.

Comprehension Check

1. Collect the target verb cards and reshuffle them.
2. Introduce the cards one by one, identifying the verbs correctly and incorrectly at random.
3. Model how to say Yes when the card is correctly identified, and No when it is incorrectly identified.

> **I:** "Buy." (Hold up the **buy** card.)
>
> **I:** "Buy. Yes." (Point to the **buy** card and nod in agreement. Motion for the learners to repeat.)
>
> **G:** "Yes."
>
> **I:** "Buy." (Hold up the **leave** card.)
>
> **I:** "Buy. No." (Point to the **leave** card and shake head in disagreement. Motion for the learners to repeat.)
>
> **G:** "No."

4. Continue with other target verbs at random.
5. Repeat words as necessary.

Oral Language Activity 3

MATERIALS

Large vocabulary cards (from Lessons A & B)

OK/Not OK cards

Yes/No cards

Pictures of a house and a car

Review the Target Vocabulary

1. Hold up each noun, verb, or adjective card and ask the group to identify each one.

> **I:** "What's this?" (Hold up the **illegal drugs** card and motion for the group to respond.)
>
> **G:** "Illegal drugs."
>
> **I:** "Good. What's this?" (Hold up the **arrest** card and motion for a response.)
>
> **G:** "Arrest."

2. Continue with other vocabulary to ensure that the group has a solid understanding of all target vocabulary from Lessons A and B.
3. Associate the vocabulary cards with the **OK** or the **Not OK** and **illegal** cards. Make sure learners understand that **leave** is an OK action, something they should do if people around them have illegal drugs.
4. Introduce sentences about illegal drugs, using the vocabulary learned in Oral Language Activities 1 and 2 and the associations with the **Not OK** and **illegal** cards, as indicated below.
5. Say each sentence and have learners repeat. Associate **Not OK** and vocabulary cards with each of the sentences to help clarify and reinforce the meaning.

Sentences about Illegal Drugs

- It's Not OK to possess illegal drugs. (Hold up the **Not OK, possess,** and **illegal drugs** cards. Hold up the **illegal** card.)
- It's Not OK to use illegal drugs. (Hold up the **Not OK, use,** and **illegal drugs** cards. Hold up the **illegal** card.)
- Illegal drug users are Not OK. (Hold up the **Not OK, illegal drugs,** and **user** cards. Hold up the **illegal** card.)
- Say NO to drugs. (Hold up the **No** card.)

6. Have learners repeat each sentence three times. If learners have difficulty repeating a sentence, break it into parts and use backward buildup to practice the parts.
7. Associate **It's Not OK to possess illegal drugs** with pictures of a car and a house to show learners that it's Not OK to possess drugs in those places as well as in public spaces.
8. Assist learners as necessary.

OK or Not OK?

1. Display the **OK, Not OK,** and **illegal** cards in a visible location at the front of the room.
2. Hold up individual cards or combinations of cards, as suggested below. Identify the word or phrase represented, and have the group decide if the behavior is OK or Not OK/illegal.
3. Use pictures as necessary to clarify the meaning of the phrase.
4. Ask the learners to repeat the terms and say whether the behaviors are OK or Not OK/illegal.
5. Use mime, pictures, and realia in addition to the cards to ensure comprehension of the terms.
6. Repeat the process as necessary for more verbal practice.

Suggested Combinations and Appropriate Responses

Sell illegal drugs = Not OK
Buy illegal drugs = Not OK
Use illegal drugs = Not OK
Possess illegal drugs = Not OK
Illegal drug users = Not OK
Leave = OK
Possess illegal drugs (in car) = Not OK
Possess illegal drugs (in house) = Not OK
Say NO = OK

Comprehension Check

1. Hold up card combinations with the **OK** or **Not OK** cards.
2. Ask learners to decide if the association with OK or Not OK is correct or incorrect.
3. Have learners respond with Yes if it is correct and No if it is not correct.

> **I:** "Possess illegal drugs. OK?" (Motion for learners to respond.)
> **G:** "No."
> **I:** "Say NO. OK?" (Motion for learners to respond.)
> **G:** "Yes."

4. Continue with various combinations to ensure that the group understands which behaviors or situations are OK and which are Not OK and illegal.

Oral Language Activity 4

MATERIALS

Large vocabulary cards

NOTE

Pointing to each word while reading is important to do even if the learners are non-readers or nonliterate.

Introduce the Dialogue

1. Write the sample dialogue (see example below) on the board or other visible surface.
2. Read through the dialogue and point to each word.
3. Use vocabulary cards, mime, and gestures as appropriate to assist the group.

> **Speaker 1:** "Should you possess illegal drugs?" (Hold up the **possess** and **illegal drugs** cards. Hold up the **illegal** card and motion for a response.)
>
> **Speaker 2:** "No, it's illegal."
>
> **Speaker 1:** "Should you use illegal drugs?" (Hold up the **use** and **illegal drugs** cards. Hold up the **illegal** card and motion for a response.)
>
> **Speaker 2:** "No, it's illegal."
>
> **Speaker 1:** "What should you do?" (Hold up the **No** card and motion for a response.)
>
> **Speaker 2:** "Say NO to drugs."
>
> **Speaker 1:** "What should you do?" (Hold up the **leave** card and motion for a response.)
>
> **Speaker 2:** "Leave."

4. Perform the dialogue as Speaker 1 and have the group respond as Speaker 2.
5. Hold up the appropriate cards to prompt learners' responses.

Dialogue Activity

1. Write the sample dialogue (see example below) on the board or on chart paper and read it for the group, pointing to each word.
2. Perform the dialogue as a group, using the written example with cards and realia to accompany each step.

> **Speaker 1:** "Should you possess illegal drugs?" (Hold up the **possess** and **illegal drugs** cards. Hold up the **illegal** card and motion for a response.)
>
> **Speaker 2:** "No, it's illegal."
>
> **Speaker 1:** "Should you use illegal drugs?" (Hold up the **use** and **drugs** cards. Hold up the **illegal** card and motion for a response.)
>
> **Speaker 2:** "No, it's illegal."
>
> **Speaker 1:** "What should you do?" (Hold up the **No** card and motion for a response.)
>
> **Speaker 2:** "Say NO to drugs."
>
> **Speaker 1:** "What should you do?" (Hold up the **leave** card and motion for a response.)
>
> **Speaker 2:** "Leave."

3. Practice the dialogue with the instructor as Speaker 1 and the group as Speaker 2.
4. Use vocabulary cards, realia, gestures, and mime as necessary to prompt the dialogue practice.
5. Assist the learners as necessary.

Comprehension Check

1. Hold up pairs of cards and identify each one. Ask the learners to point to the card that represents an illegal behavior, identify the card, and say that it is illegal.

> **I:** "Take LSD. Leave." (Hold up the **LSD** and **leave** cards, and motion for the learners to choose the illegal behavior. Have the learners point to that card and respond.)
>
> **G:** "Take LSD. Illegal." (Point to the **LSD** card.)
>
> **I:** "Medicine. Buy cocaine/crack." (Hold up the **medicine** and **cocaine/crack** cards and motion for the learners to choose the illegal behavior. Have the learners point to that card and respond.)
>
> **G:** "Buy cocaine/crack. Illegal." (Point to the **cocaine/crack** card.)

2. Show various pairs to ensure that the group has a solid understanding of what is legal and what is illegal.
3. Repeat problematic pairs as necessary, assisting learners.

Reading Activity

Review

1. Shuffle all of the target vocabulary cards.
2. Show each card to the group while pronouncing each word slowly and clearly.
3. Run a finger under each word to help learners begin to recognize the words apart from the pictures.
4. Have the learners repeat the nouns or verbs at least three times.

> **I:** "Possess." (Point to the word.)
>
> **G:** "Possess."
>
> **I:** "Possess." (Underline the word with a finger. Motion for the group to repeat the word.)
>
> **G:** "Possess."

MATERIALS

Large vocabulary cards

Circle the Correct Word activity sheet (one enlarged and one per learner)

5. Continue to review with the cards, using the previous pattern.
6. Fold cards in half to show only the words, to help learners become less dependent on the pictures.
7. Move from group to individual practice as learners become more comfortable reading the words without the assistance of the pictures.

Circle the Correct Word Activity

1. Display the large vocabulary cards from Lesson B in a visible location for learners' reference.
2. Distribute a Circle the Correct Word activity sheet to each learner.
3. Post an enlarged activity sheet in the front of the room or in another visible location.
4. Using the enlarged activity sheet, ask learners to look at and identify each picture.
5. Use the example to show learners how to complete the activity sheet.
6. Help learners to use the large vocabulary cards to match the picture in the example to one of the words listed next to the picture.
7. On the enlarged activity sheet, demonstrate how to find the word that corresponds to the picture.
8. On the example item, show learners how to circle the word that corresponds to the picture.
9. Complete the activity sheet as a group.

Writing Activity

Review

1. Shuffle all of the target vocabulary cards.
2. Show each card to the group while pronouncing each word slowly and clearly.
3. Run a finger under each word to help learners begin to recognize the words apart from the pictures.
4. Have the learners repeat the nouns or verbs at least three times.

> **I:** "Leave." (Point to the word.)
> **G:** "Leave."
> **I:** "Leave." (Underline the word with a finger. Motion for the group to repeat the word.)
> **G:** "Leave."

5. Continue to review with the cards, using the pattern above.
6. Fold cards in half to show only the words, to help learners become less dependent on the pictures.
7. Move from group to individual practice as learners become more comfortable reading the words without the assistance of the pictures.

Drug Information Activity

1. Display the large vocabulary cards from Lesson B in a visible location for learners' reference.
2. Distribute a Drug Information activity sheet to each learner.
3. Post an enlarged activity sheet in the front of the room or in another visible location.
4. Using the enlarged activity sheet, ask learners to look at and identify each picture.
5. Write the names of illegal drugs (marijuana, cocaine/crack, ecstasy, and LSD) on the board or on chart paper. Point to each one and have learners read it.
6. Using an example item on the enlarged activity sheet, demonstrate to learners how to write the name of a drug next to the corresponding picture.
7. Have learners look at their activity sheets and write the name of each drug on the line next to the corresponding picture.
8. Point to the **leave, No,** and **illegal drugs** cards where they are displayed.
9. Have learners write *leave* on the line next to the corresponding picture and fill in the missing words to complete the sentence *Say NO to illegal drugs* next to the picture of illegal drugs.
10. Have volunteers come to the front and write the remaining words on the enlarged activity sheet. Alternatively, point to each line and have learners read from their own sheets to tell you what word to write there.

3 Unit Review Activity

MATERIALS

Unit Review activity sheet (one enlarged and one per learner)

Large vocabulary cards (from Lessons A & B)

Medicine bottles and packages (prescription and over-the-counter)

Pictures of prescription and over-the-counter medicine and illegal drugs

NOTE

The Unit Review Activity can be done as a group activity for reinforcing the concepts learned in the lesson or done as an individual activity for assessment purposes.

Unit Review Activities

1. Use the large vocabulary cards from Lessons A and B, along with realia and pictures, to review the vocabulary and concepts from the Unit.
2. Focus on having learners identify different types of drugs and medicine (prescription, over the-counter, and illegal).
3. Distribute a copy of the Unit Review activity sheet to each learner. Post an enlarged copy of the activity sheet in the front of the room.
4. On the enlarged activity sheet, point to each picture and have learners identify the type of medicine or drug. Point to the words at the tops of the columns and have learners read the terms. If necessary, say each term while pointing to it and have learners repeat.
5. Ask learners to complete the activity at the top of the page. If necessary, use the enlarged activity sheet to model checking the appropriate column.
6. Review the pictures at the bottom of the page. Point to each one and ask learners if it is OK or Not OK (illegal). Model how to circle one of the drugs that learners identify as illegal.
7. Ask learners to complete the activity on their own sheets.
8. Have volunteers come to the front and on the enlarged sheet, circle the other illegal drugs.
9. Assist learners as necessary.

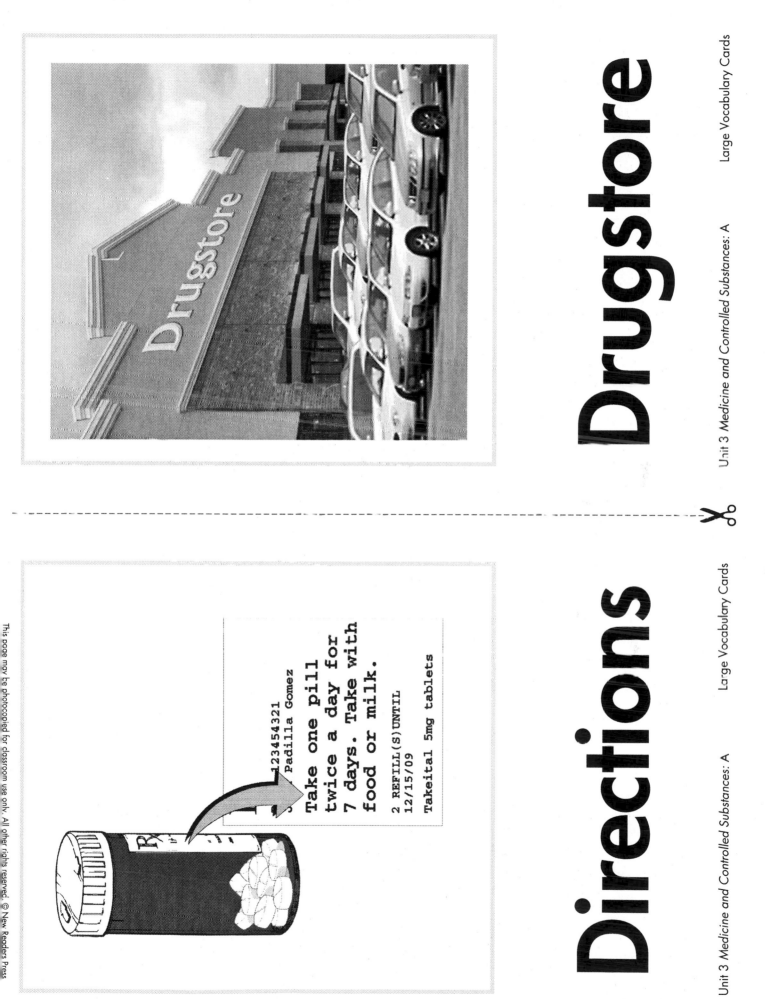

Drugstore

123454321
Padilla Gomez

Take one pill
twice a day for
7 days. Take with
food or milk.

2 REFILL(S)UNTIL
12/15/09

Takeital 5mg tablets

Directions

Medicine

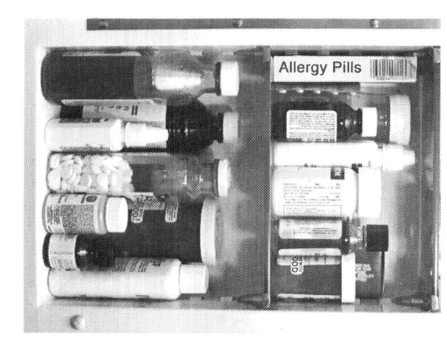

Pharmacy

Over-the-counter

Supermarket

Prescription

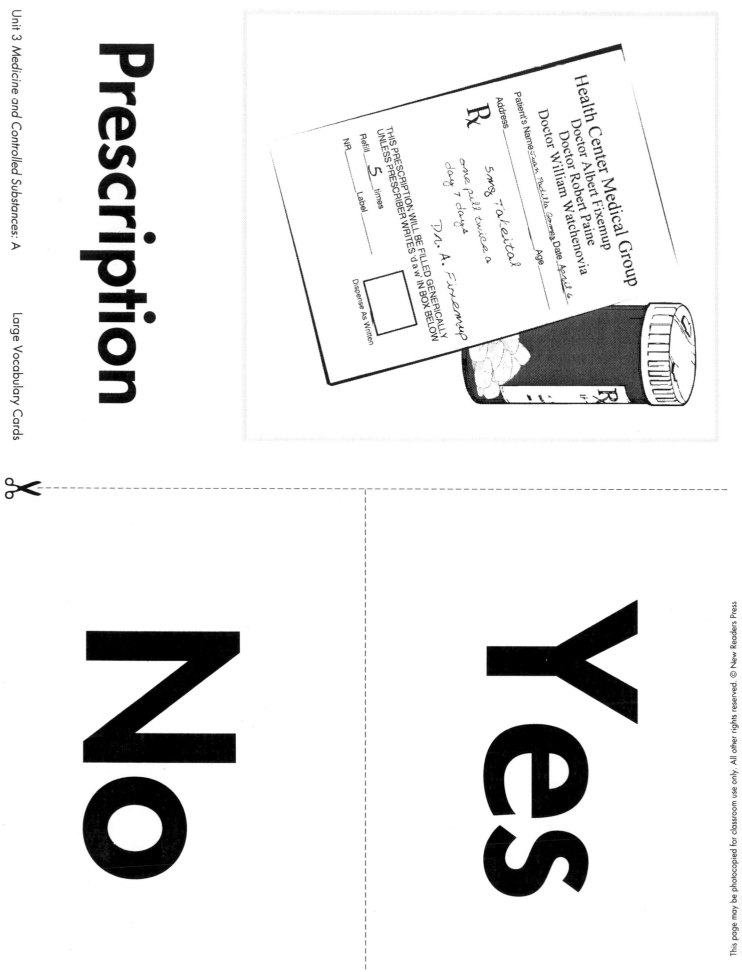

Health Center Medical Group
Doctor Albert Fixemup
Doctor Robert Paine
Doctor William Watchenovia

Patient's Name Juan Padilla Gomez Date April 6

Address _____ Age _____

℞

5mg Taleital
one pill twice a
day 7 days

Dr. A. Fixemup

THIS PRESCRIPTION WILL BE FILLED GENERICALLY
UNLESS PRESCRIBER WRITES 'd a w IN BOX BELOW

Refill __5__ times   Label _____

NR _____

Dispense As Written

Yes

No

Doctor

Unit 3 *Medicine and Controlled Substances: A*

Large Vocabulary Cards

Picture Bingo Board 1

Picture Bingo Board 2

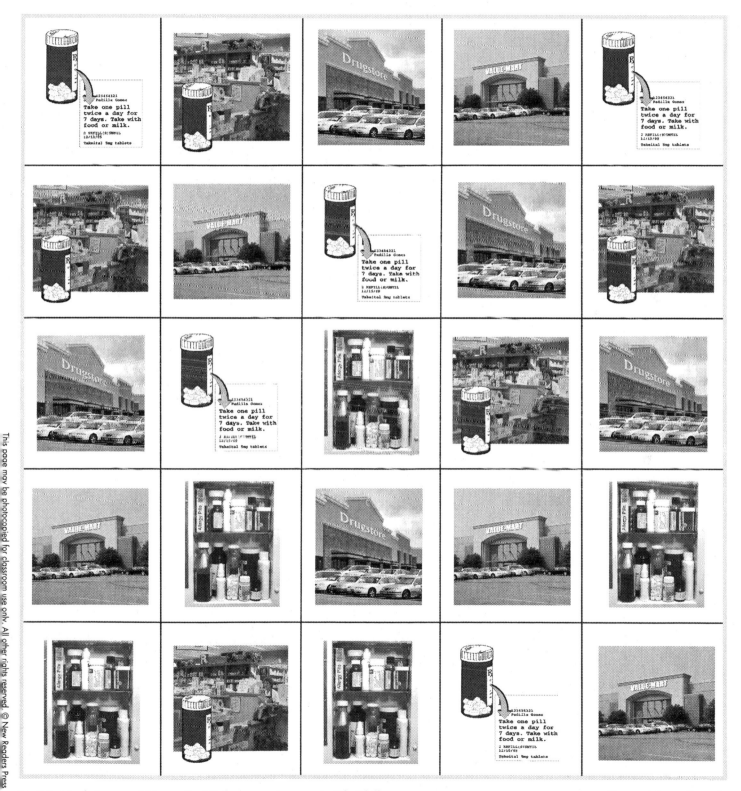

Picture Bingo Board 3

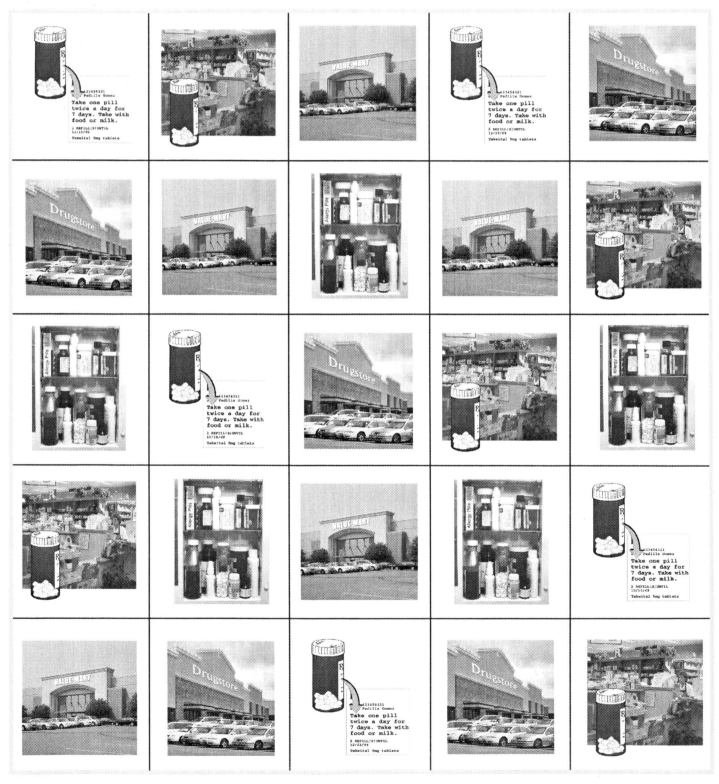

Picture Bingo Board 4

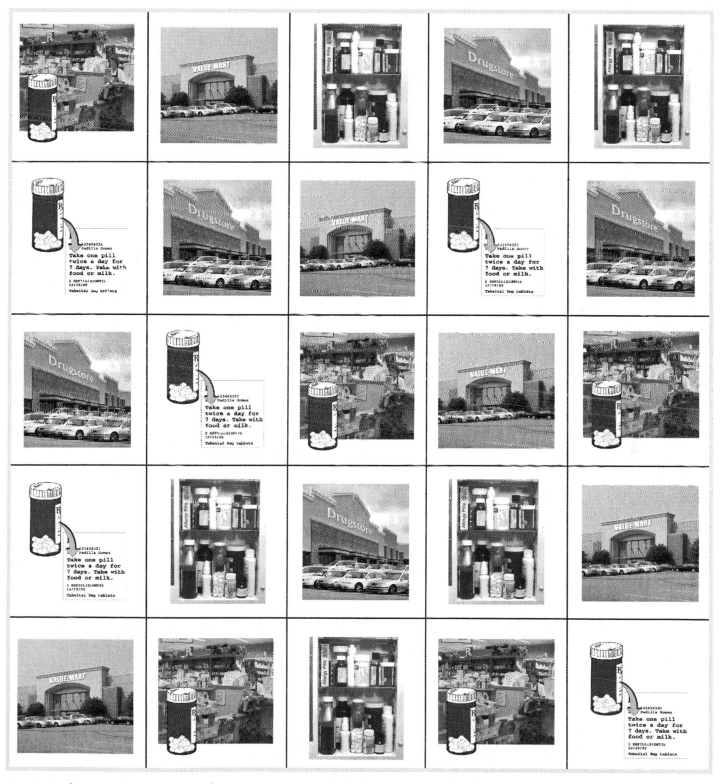

Unit 3 *Medicine and Controlled Substances* Lesson A *Life Skill*

Picture Bingo Boards

Small Doctor Cards

Word Search Activity

Look at the pictures. Find the words hidden in the puzzle. Circle the hidden words.

| Directions | Drugstore | Medicine | Pharmacy | Supermarket |

w	s	h	d	l	k	l	p	h	a	r	m	a	c	y	q	n	m	h
o	m	e	d	i	c	i	n	e	u	b	t	s	f	s	y	n	a	d
n	b	s	d	i	p	n	p	a	a	i	n	g	u	q	i	e	m	k
t	e	b	e	i	s	u	p	e	r	m	a	r	k	e	t	x	f	n
u	c	o	h	v	b	n	i	d	r	u	g	s	t	o	r	e	k	g
p	f	h	p	z	d	t	a	s	w	l	t	a	k	s	x	m	e	o
t	h	u	a	d	i	r	e	c	t	i	o	n	s	f	t	u	d	o
e	a	f	h	u	y	a	a	l	e	t	y	o	p	z	t	f	a	l

Unit 3 *Medicine and Controlled Substances* Lesson A *Life Skill*

Reading Activity Sheet

Fill in the Missing Words Activity

Look at each picture. Write the missing words on the lines.

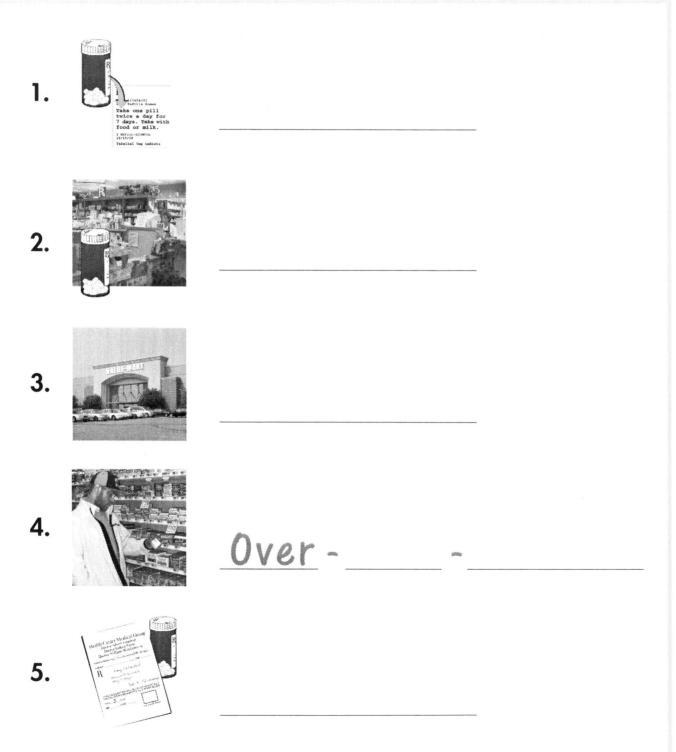

1. _____

2. _____

3. _____

4. Over - _____ - _____

5. _____

Unit 3 *Medicine and Controlled Substances* Lesson A *Life Skill*

Writing Activity Sheet

Ecstacy

Illegal Drugs

Cocaine/ Crack

✂ -

LSD

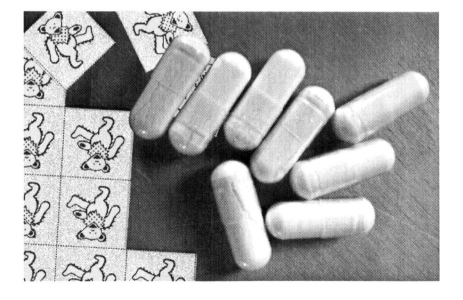

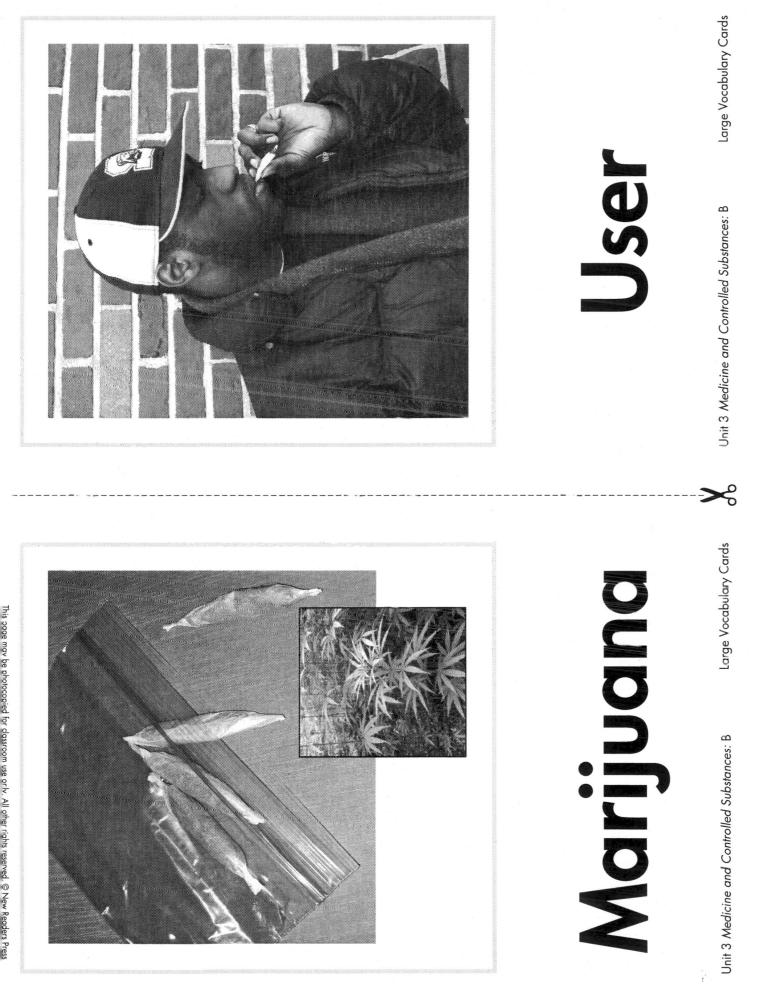

User

Unit 3 *Medicine and Controlled Substances: B*

Marijuana

Unit 3 *Medicine and Controlled Substances: B*

Arrest

Buy

Possess

Unit 3 *Medicine and Controlled Substances:* B

✂

Leave

Unit 3 *Medicine and Controlled Substances:* B

Sell

Use

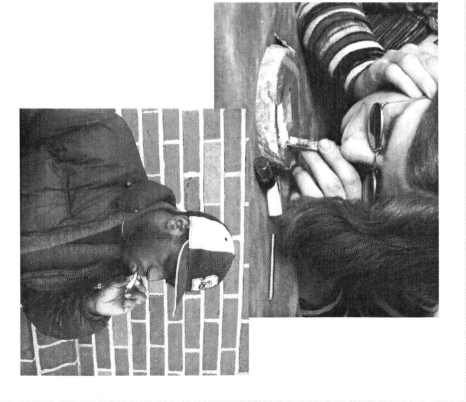

Illegal

Unit 3 Medicine and Controlled Substances: B

Large Vocabulary Cards

Circle the Correct Word Activity

Look at the pictures. Circle the correct words.

	Use	Possess	(Illegal drugs)
	LSD	Ecstasy	Marijuana
	Cocaine	User	Sell
	Buy	Sell	Arrest
	Possess	Use	Arrest
	Sell	Marijuana	Illegal drugs
	Leave	Illegal	Use

Reading Activity Sheet

Drug Information Activity

Look at the pictures. Write the words on the lines. Fill in the missing words for a message about drugs.

 _____

 _____

 _____

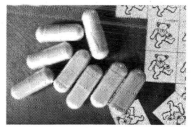 _____

 _____

Say _____ to _____ _____.

Look at each picture. Check Over-the-counter or Prescription for each medicine.

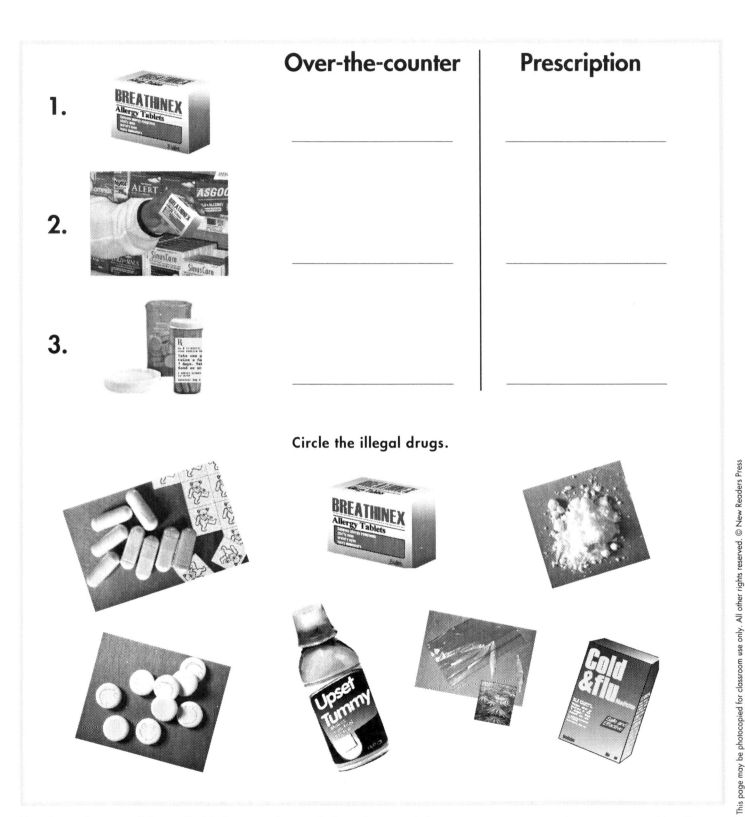

	Over-the-counter	Prescription
1.	_____	_____
2.	_____	_____
3.	_____	_____

Circle the illegal drugs.

Unit 4

Having Safe Relationships

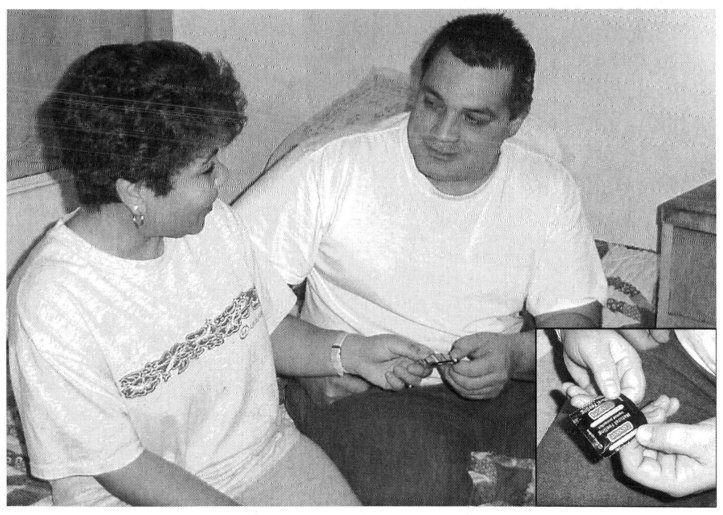

Lesson A - Life Skill

Safe Sex

VOCABULARY

NOUNS

Disease

Latex condom

Man

Pregnancy

Sex

Woman

VERBS

Choose

Use

QUESTION

What should you choose?

Objectives

- To help learners understand the dangers associated with at-risk sexual behavior
- To enable learners to make informed and safe choices about sexual behavior

Adapting Lesson Activities

The information and vocabulary in this lesson may be most suitable for single, young-adult learners (or single learners of any age). In addition, the lesson deals with matters that learners who are parents, particularly parents of teens, need to understand. The issues surrounding safe sex are also important for individuals in relationships with partners who may be sexually active outside their relationships. At the same time, recognize and be sensitive to the differing needs of learners in committed, monogamous relationships, particularly those who regard pregnancy as a desirable outcome, rather than as the undesirable risk presented in this lesson.

Learners' cultural backgrounds should also be considered when introducing this lesson. Some learners may be uncomfortable dealing with the subject matter in a public setting. In addition, many women learners will find it impossible to address the unit's issues in a mixed-gender class. You might decide to teach men and women separately.

If your learners have varied needs and concerns, it may be more effective to teach this unit outside of regular class time. You may choose to teach it only to students for whom it is appropriate.

Materials Included

- Central theme picture
- Large reproducible vocabulary cards
- Graphic Organizer activity sheet
- Write the Dialogue activity sheet
- Picture Bingo boards
- **Yes/No** cards

Materials Needed

- Pictures of couples, men, women, and pregnant women
- A package of latex condoms
- Latex glove(s)
- Can and can opener, pencil and pencil sharpener, paper and pen, or small household or cooking tool
- A medical book or illustrated encyclopedia
- Bingo board markers (paper clips, buttons, dried beans, coins, or other small objects)
- Additional instructor copy (enlarged) of the activity sheets
- Pictures of various food items or drinks

Central Theme Picture

MATERIALS

Theme picture

Introduce the Theme Picture

1. Show learners the theme picture and ask for a response.
2. Encourage learners to say anything about the picture that they can.

POSSIBLE RESPONSES

Bed/Bedroom

Condom

Give

Man

Talking

Woman

> **I:** "What's happening in this picture?" (Point out key things about the picture to elicit a response.)

Oral Language Activity 1

MATERIALS

Large noun cards

Theme picture

Pictures of men, women, and pregnant women

Medical books or illustrated encyclopedias

Latex glove(s)

A package of latex condoms

Picture Bingo boards (enlarged, if possible, for greater clarity)

Introduce the Target Nouns

1. Show each large noun card to the group, pronouncing each word slowly and clearly, and motion for learners to repeat.
2. Use pictures and realia to clarify and reinforce the meaning of the target nouns (see suggestions below).

> **I:** "Man." (Hold up the **man** card. Show a picture of a man from a magazine. Motion for learners to repeat.)
> **G:** "Man."
> **I:** "Good. Man." (Motion for learners to repeat.)
> **G:** "Man."
> **I:** "Very good. What's this?" (Hold up the **man** card. Motion for a response.)
> **G:** "Man."

3. Use the format above to introduce the other target nouns (**disease, woman, latex condom, sex,** and **pregnancy**).
4. Point out to learners the symbols for **man** and **woman** on those vocabulary cards. If possible, ask learners to say where they have seen those symbols (e.g., on public bathroom doors).

Suggestions for Pictures and Realia

Disease - medical book or encyclopedia that illustrates various diseases

Man, Woman - pictures of men and of women

Latex condom - a latex glove to illustrate latex as a material, a package of condoms

Pregnancy - pictures of pregnant women from magazines

5. Have all learners repeat each word three times.

Picture Bingo Activity

1. Distribute one Picture Bingo board and a set of markers to each learner.
2. Show learners how to win with five pictures in a row (horizontally, vertically, or diagonally).
3. Shuffle the large noun cards and place them in a pile.
4. Choose a card, show it to the learners, and have them identify the card verbally.
5. Demonstrate how to find the chosen word on a Bingo board and how to mark it with a small marker.
6. Ask learners to say the word again as they mark it on their boards.
7. Have learners repeat each word as the boards are marked.

> **I:** "What's this?" (Hold up the **pregnancy** card and motion for a response.)
>
> **G:** "Pregnancy."
>
> **I:** "Great. Pregnancy." (Show learners how to find **pregnancy** on the board and how to mark it. Motion for them to repeat the word.)
>
> **G:** "Pregnancy."

8. Continue the activity until a learner has five pictures marked in a row (horizontally, vertically, or diagonally).
9. Have learners call out *Bingo* if they have five in a row marked on their board.
10. When a learner has Bingo, rotate the boards and repeat the activity for additional practice.
11. Assist learners as necessary.

Comprehension Check

1. Place the large noun cards faceup on a table or other visible surface.
2. Say a word at random. Have learners repeat the word and try to point to the corresponding card.

> **I:** "Pregnancy." (Motion for the group to repeat.)
>
> **G:** "Pregnancy." (Point to the **pregnancy** card.)

3. Ask the learner who points to the card first repeat the word individually.
4. Repeat words as necessary to ensure the group's comprehension of the terms.

Oral Language Activity 2

Introduce the Verbs

1. Introduce the verb **choose** by using pictures of various food items or drinks.
2. Hold up two pictures, showing similar items (e.g., a cup of tea and a cup of coffee or two different types of fruit) and demonstrate the verb **choose.**

> **I:** "Choose." (Use mime and gesture to demonstrate making a choice between two food or drink choices. Motion for learners to repeat.)
>
> **G:** "Choose."
>
> **I:** "Good. Choose." (Point to the two pictures. Hold up one of them. Motion for learners to repeat together.)
>
> **G:** "Choose."
>
> **I:** "Very good. Choose." (Motion for the group to repeat.)
>
> **G:** "Choose."

3. Introduce the verb **use** by demonstrating using a simple tool (e.g., by opening a can with a can opener, sharpening a pencil, writing words on paper with a pencil or pen, or showing use of a simple household tool, such as a hammer or a simple cooking tool).
4. Have learners repeat each verb at least three times.
5. Make sure that the learners understand the meanings of the verbs before continuing on to the activity.

Verb TPR (Total Physical Response)

1. Place the pictures and realia used to introduce the verbs **choose** and **use** on the table or on another visible surface.
2. Demonstrate to the group that they will listen for each verb and pick up appropriate pictures or realia to act out the verb.

> **I:** "Choose." (Hold a hand with palm open up to an ear to signal the group to listen.)
>
> **I:** "Choose." (Demonstrate making a choice between two pictured food items or drinks {e.g., tea or coffee, bread or a roll}. Motion for the group to repeat.)
>
> **G:** "Choose."
>
> **I:** "Choose." (Demonstrate making a choice between two food items or drinks, as above. Motion for the group to repeat.)
>
> **G:** "Choose."

3. Model **use** following a similar format. Demonstrate using a simple tool (e.g., by opening a can with a can opener, sharpening a pencil, writing words on paper with a pencil or pen, or showing use of a simple household tool, such as a hammer or a simple cooking tool).
4. Call on a learner or learners or ask for volunteers, and specify which verb to demonstrate with the pictures and realia. Have the learner(s) repeat the verb after the demonstration.
5. Vary having learners demonstrate **choose** or **use** at random.
6. Have the group say each verb after it has been demonstrated by a learner or learners.
7. Assist the group as necessary.

Comprehension Check

1. Demonstrate the verbs **choose** and **use** by using the realia and mimed actions suggested above.
2. Ask learners to orally identify which verb is being demonstrated.

> **I:** "What's this?" (Mime opening a can with a can opener or sharpening a pencil with a sharpener. Motion for a response.)
>
> **G:** "Use."

3. Act out **choose** or **use** at random, to avoid predictability in the response.
4. Ask learners, as a group or individually, to identify each verb.

Oral Language Activity 3

MATERIALS

Large vocabulary cards

Theme picture

Yes/No cards (multiple copies of the **No** card)

Review the Target Vocabulary

1. Hold up each large vocabulary card and motion for the group to respond.

> **I:** "What's this?" (Hold up the **woman** card and motion for a response.)
>
> **G:** "Woman."
>
> **I:** "What's this?" (Hold up the **latex condom** card and motion for a response.)
>
> **G:** "Latex condom."

2. Continue with other vocabulary following the format above, to ensure the group's understanding of the terms.
3. Use mime and gestures to elicit the target verbs (**use** and **choose**).
4. Repeat prompts as necessary.

NOTE

The purpose of this activity is to help the group understand choices and consequences for safe sex vs. unprotected sex. (You may also wish to help learners understand that latex condoms are not 100% foolproof.)

It may be helpful to prepare a separate set of vocabulary cards (using cards for **sex, disease, pregnancy,** and **latex condom**) with the No symbol (circle with diagonal line) over the picture and the word No written next to the vocabulary word on the card.

Create a Graphic Organizer

1. Prepare learners to make a graphic organizer by having them identify each of the terms that will need to be used.

> **I:** "No sex." (Hold up the **No** and **sex** cards. Motion for the group to repeat the term.)
>
> **G:** "No sex."
>
> **I:** "Latex condom." (Hold up the **latex condom** card. Hold up the theme picture and point to the latex condom package. Motion for the group to respond.)
>
> **G:** "Latex condom."
>
> **I:** "Choose no sex." (Hold up the **No** and **sex** cards. Motion for the group to repeat.)
>
> **G:** "Choose no sex."
>
> **I:** "Choose latex condom." (Hold up the **latex condom** card. Point to the latex condom in the theme picture. Motion for the group to repeat.)
>
> **G:** "Choose latex condom."

2. Display the **No** and **sex** cards (paired) and the **latex condom** card on a table or posted on a wall or on chart paper.

3. Present the result of these choices to the group by introducing the terms for the results (*no disease* and *no pregnancy*) using the method above.

4. Place the appropriate cards for results next to the choices (**No sex** and **latex condom**). Draw arrows between the choices and the associated results to create the first part of a graphic organizer (see example below).

> **I:** "No disease." (Hold up the **No** and **disease** cards. Motion for the group to repeat the term.)
>
> **G:** "No disease."
>
> **I:** "No pregnancy." (Hold up the **No** and **pregnancy** cards. Motion for the group to repeat the term.)
>
> **G:** "No pregnancy."
>
> **I:** "Choose no sex. No disease. No pregnancy." (Point to the first choice and the results. Ask the group to repeat each term one by one.)
>
> **G:** "Choose no sex. No disease. No pregnancy."
>
> **I:** "Choose latex condom. No disease. No pregnancy." (Point to the second choice and the results. Ask the group to repeat each term one by one.)
>
> **G:** "Choose latex condom. No disease. No pregnancy."

5. Use the method above to introduce the choice of **No latex condom.** Associate this with the results **disease** and **pregnancy.**

6. Display the cards for **No latex condom** under the choices presented previously. Place the cards for the results (**disease** and **pregnancy**) next to the choice of **No latex condom.**
7. Have the learners repeat each term at least three times.
8. Have the group associate choices with the correct corresponding results.
9. Use the method above to teach the phrase, **use latex condom.** Associate that with the results of **No disease** and **No pregnancy.**
10. Help learners understand that if they do choose sex, they should use a latex condom. Show the theme picture and point to the latex condom. Post the **sex** card next to the **latex condom** card on the board or on chart paper and put a plus (+) sign between them.
11. Assist learners as necessary.

Suggested Graphic Organizer

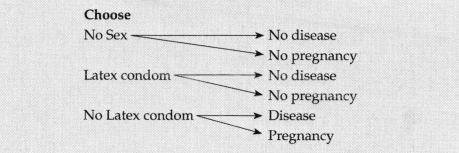

Choose

No Sex ⟶ No disease / No pregnancy

Latex condom ⟶ No disease / No pregnancy

No Latex condom ⟶ Disease / Pregnancy

Comprehension Check

1. Hold up correct and incorrect pairings of choices and results.
2. Have learners identify if the combination of choice and result is paired correctly (Yes) or incorrectly (No).

> **I:** "No latex condom. Disease." (Point to the **No** and **latex condom** cards and the **disease** card as they are identified. Hold up the **Yes** and **No** cards and motion for a response.)
>
> **G:** "Yes." (Learners should point to the **Yes** card.)
>
> **I:** "Latex condom. Disease." (Point to the **latex condom** and **disease** cards as they are identified. Hold up the **Yes** and **No** cards and motion for a response.)
>
> **G:** "No." (Learners should point to the **No** card.)

3. Continue with other correct and incorrect pairings to help ensure learners' comprehension of the choices and results and of their connection.

Oral Language Activity 4

MATERIALS

Large vocabulary cards (two sets)

No card (multiple copies)

Theme picture

A package of latex condoms

OK/Not OK cards

NOTE

Pointing to each word while reading is important to do even if the learners are nonreaders or non-literate.

Introduce the Dialogue

1. Write model question/answer pairs for the dialogue (see example below) on the board or on another visible surface.
2. Go through the dialogue, pronouncing each question/answer pair clearly for the group. Refer to the question/answer pairs by pointing to each line while holding up the cards and any associated pictures or realia to prompt the answer.

> **Speaker 1:** "What do you choose?" (Hold up the **No** and **disease** cards.)
>
> **Speaker 2:** "No disease."
>
> **Speaker 1:** "What do you choose?" (Hold up the **No** and **pregnancy** cards.)
>
> **Speaker 2:** "No pregnancy."
>
> **Speaker 1:** "What do you choose?" (Hold up the **No** and **sex** cards.)
>
> **Speaker 2:** "No sex."
>
> **Speaker 1:** "What do you choose?" (Hold up the **latex condom** card. Show a package of latex condoms and/or point to the condom package in the theme picture.)
>
> **Speaker 2:** "Latex condom."

3. If appropriate, add an exchange to associate the term **latex condom** with the verb **use.**

> **Speaker 1:** "What do you use?" (Hold up the **sex** and **latex condom** cards.)
>
> **Speaker 2:** "Latex condom."

4. Practice the dialogue with the instructor taking the role of Speaker 1 and learners taking the role of Speaker 2.
5. If necessary, model the responses for learners and have them repeat.
6. Make sure that the learners can respond to each verbal and visual prompt before continuing on to the dialogue activity.

Dialogue Activity

1. Review the question/answer pairs from the dialogue. Ask the question and prompt learners visually using cards and realia as appropriate for the desired response.
2. If necessary, assist learners by modeling the response and having them repeat.

> **I:** "What do you choose?" (Hold up the **No** and **disease** cards.)
>
> **G:** "No disease."

3. Continue with the activity by prompting learners visually and verbally using cards, and if desired, by showing appropriate realia or pictures.

> **I:** "What do you choose?" (Hold up the **No** and **pregnancy** cards.)
>
> **G:** "No pregnancy."
>
> **I:** "What do you choose?" (Hold up the **No** and **sex** cards.)
>
> **G:** "No sex."
>
> **I:** "What do you choose?" (Hold up the **latex condom** card.)
>
> **G:** "Latex condom."

4. Repeat the couplets by holding up individual or paired cards in random order to prompt learners' responses.
5. Assist the group as necessary.

Comprehension Check

1. Display one set of the large vocabulary cards faceup on the table or on another available surface. Group some cards with a **No** card, as indicated below.
2. Using a second set of the large vocabulary cards, prompt learners by holding up cards or cards paired with a **No** card.

Cards to Display

No pregnancy	Disease
No disease	Pregnancy
No sex	No latex condom
Latex condom	

> **I:** "What do you choose?" (Hold up the **No** and **disease** cards. Motion for the group to find these cards.)
>
> **G:** "No disease." (Point to the **No** and **disease** cards.)
>
> **I:** "OK or Not OK?" (Hold up the **OK** and **Not OK** cards. Motion for learners to respond and point to the appropriate card.)
>
> **G:** "OK."

3. Continue to ask the group to respond to verbal and visual prompts using the vocabulary cards. Check comprehension by asking if the choice is OK or Not OK.

4. When **disease, pregnancy,** and **No latex condom** are given as choices, make sure that learners point to the **Not OK** card.

Reading Activity

Review

MATERIALS

Large noun cards

Graphic Organizer activity sheet (one enlarged and one per learner)

1. Shuffle all of the target vocabulary cards.
2. Show each card to the group while pronouncing each word slowly and clearly.
3. Run a finger under each word to help learners begin to recognize the words apart from the pictures.
4. Have the learners repeat the words at least three times.

> **I:** "Pregnancy." (Point to the word.)
>
> **G:** "Pregnancy."
>
> **I:** "Pregnancy." (Underline the word with a finger. Motion for the group to repeat the word.)
>
> **G:** "Pregnancy."

NOTE

Separating words from pictures should be done gradually and after plenty of practice.

5. Continue to review with the cards, using the pattern above.
6. Fold cards in half to show only the words, to help learners become less dependent on the pictures.
7. Move from group to individual practice as learners become more comfortable reading the words without the assistance of the pictures.

Graphic Organizer Activity

1. Display the large vocabulary cards in a visible location for learners' reference.
2. Distribute a Graphic Organizer activity sheet to each learner.
3. Post an enlarged activity sheet in the front of the room or in another visible location.
4. Using the enlarged activity sheet, ask learners to look at and identify each picture.
5. Model for learners how to read the graphic organizer. Point to the first picture and trace the arrows to the results. Then model saying the phrases corresponding to the pictures. Use the verbs **choose** and **use** for the choices in the left column.

> **I:** "Choose no sex. No disease. Choose no sex. No pregnancy. (Point to the appropriate pictures and trace the connecting arrows while saying the phrases.)

6. Repeat for each set of choices and results.

7. Say the phrases corresponding to the pictures while pointing and tracing the arrows. Motion for learners to repeat each paired choice and result.
8. Read through the activity sheet as a group.
9. Check learners' understanding by pointing to a choice picture and saying what it is. Then trace an arrow to one of the results and have learners read that result.
10. Ask volunteers to come to the front and point and trace a paired choice and result while saying the corresponding phrases.

Writing Activity

Materials

Large noun cards

Write the Dialogue activity sheet (one enlarged and one per learner)

Review

1. Shuffle all of the target vocabulary cards.
2. Show each card to the group while pronouncing each word slowly and clearly.
3. Run a finger under each word to help learners begin to recognize the words apart from the pictures.
4. Have the learners repeat the words at least three times.

> **I:** "Man." (Point to the word.)
> **G:** "Man."
> **I:** "Man." (Underline the word with a finger. Motion for the group to repeat the word.)
> **G:** "Man."

NOTE

Separating words from pictures should be done gradually and after plenty of practice.

5. Continue to review with the cards, using the pattern above.
6. Fold cards in half to show only the words, to help learners become less dependent on the pictures.
7. Move from group to individual practice as learners become more comfortable reading the words without the assistance of the pictures.

Write the Dialogue Activity

1. Distribute a Write the Dialogue activity sheet to each learner.
2. Place an enlarged copy of the activity sheet at the front of the room or another visible location.
3. Display the large vocabulary cards in a visible location for learners' reference.
4. Read the question in the role of Speaker 1. Ask learners to look at each picture and respond in the role of Speaker 2 with the appropriate phrase from the dialogue.

5. Using the enlarged copy of the activity sheet, demonstrate where and how to write the phrases on the correct lines on the activity sheet.
6. Have learners complete their own activity sheets.
7. Assist learners as necessary.

Lesson B - Civic Responsibility

Age of Consent

VOCABULARY

NOUNS
Adult

Age

ID

Minor

VERB & VERB PHRASES
Check

Check ID

Give consent

ADJECTIVES
Illegal

Legal

PREPOSITIONS
Over

Under

SENTENCES
Sex with a minor is illegal.

It is illegal for a minor to say Yes.

Objective

To ensure that learners understand that it is illegal to have sexual relationships with minors, even though a minor may give consent

Adapting Lesson Activities

The information and vocabulary in this lesson may be most suitable for single, young-adult learners (or single learners of any age). But the lesson deals with matters that learners who are parents, particularly parents of teens, need to understand. The legal implications of age of consent are covered in the Civics Introduction on page 179.

Although the legal age of consent varies from state to state and even from place to place within a state, these lesson notes refer to 18 as the age of consent for consistency and simplicity. Check the legal age in your area and, if different, substitute your local age in the lesson activities.

Materials Included

- Large reproducible vocabulary cards
- ID cards with ages over and under 18
- Circle the Correct Word activity sheet
- Write the Dialogue activity sheet
- **Over/Under** cards
- **Yes/No** cards
- **OK/Not OK** cards (page 208)

Materials Needed

- Pictures of adults, teenagers, and children
- Real or instructor-made replicas of identification cards that include date of birth or other indication of age (driver's license, school ID, etc.)
- Instructor-made age cards
- Additional instructor copy (enlarged) of the activity sheets

Civics Introduction

Age of Consent

In the U.S., the age of consent for sexual activity differs from state to state, and sometimes from locality to locality. Knowing the legal age of consent is important for both men and women not only because it is a sensitive issue, but because variations among laws in different places can make this issue difficult to understand. Adults need to understand laws regulating age of consent not just for themselves but also for their children.

In most places, age of consent law is violated in the case of sex between an adult and an individual who has not reached that location's legal age. In some places, age of consent law can also be violated by two minors. Violating age of consent law is a crime, considered anything from a relatively low-level misdemeanor to statutory rape, which can carry the same legal consequences as the crime of rape.

This issue is important to newly arrived, non-English-speaking adults and their families because the laws in the U.S. may differ from those in their native countries, and thus may be particularly difficult to understand. The issue is especially important because the consequences of violating laws regulating age of consent can be quite severe in the U.S.

Oral Language Activity 1

MATERIALS

Two sets of large noun cards (from Lessons A & B)

Yes/No cards (one set per learner)

Introduce the Target Nouns

1. Show each large noun card to the group while pronouncing each word slowly and clearly.

> **I:** "Age." (Hold up the **age** card. Motion for the group to repeat together.)
>
> **G:** "Age."
>
> **I:** "Good. Age." (Motion for the group to repeat.)
>
> **G:** "Age."
>
> **I:** "Age." (Motion for the group to repeat.)
>
> **G:** "Age."

NOTE

If a learner is uncomfortable or sensitive about telling his or her age for any reason, don't press the issue. Simply move on to the next learner.

2. Post the **age** card on the board or on chart paper. Make sure there is plenty of room to write below the card.
3. Tell the group your age. Ask each learner his or her age.
4. Write all of the ages in a visible location under the **age** card. (Save a copy of this list to use in Oral Language Activity 2, when explaining the concepts of **over** and **under**.)

NOTE

The legal definition of *minor* will be covered in Oral Language Activity 2.

5. Introduce the other target nouns (**ID, adult,** and **minor**) using the method above and showing appropriate realia (see suggestions below).

Suggestions for realia

ID—show real or instructor-made replicas of identification cards that include date of birth or other indication of age (driver's license, school ID, etc.) or use the ID cards provided for this lesson

Adult—show learners pictures of men and women and give an approximate age for each (depending on the picture), identifying each person as 18 or over

Minor—show learners pictures of young (teen-aged) men and women and of children. Give an approximate age for each (depending on the picture), identifying each person as under 18

6. Say each word and have the group repeat each one three times.
7. Review the nouns from Lesson A by showing the cards and eliciting a response from the group.
8. Repeat any words more than three times as necessary (with the group, with pairs, or individually).

NOTE

Photocopying each set of noun cards on a different color of paper will help to facilitate the matching of pairs.

Concentration

1. Shuffle the two sets of large noun cards (from Lessons A and B).
2. Place each card facedown on a table or other surface, making sure the cards do not overlap.
3. Turn over one card and identify it for the group.

4. Demonstrate the activity by turning over another card in search of a matched pair.
5. Model getting a matched pair to show how a player with a matched pair keeps the cards and is allowed an extra turn.
6. Model getting cards that do not match to show how those cards must be put back facedown on the table.
7. Show the learners one success and one failure of finding a matched pair, to help them understand the purpose of the activity.
8. Encourage learners to identify both cards verbally as they are selected.
9. Hold the cards that are difficult for the group until the end of the activity and repeat them.

Comprehension Check

1. Distribute a set of **Yes/No** cards to each learner.
2. Hold up a large vocabulary card and identify it correctly.
3. Motion for the group to hold up a **Yes** or **No** card.

> **I:** "Adult." (Hold up the **adult** card and/or magazine pictures of adults. Motion for a response.)
>
> **G:** "Yes." (Hold up the **Yes** card.)

4. Hold up a large vocabulary card and identify it incorrectly.
5. Motion for the group to hold up a **Yes** or **No** card.

> **I:** "Minor." (Hold up the **adult** card and/or magazine pictures of adults. Motion for a response.)
>
> **G:** "No." (Hold up the **No** card.)

6. Continue with other nouns, identifying them correctly and incorrectly at random.
7. Have learners hold up the **Yes** card if the noun is identified correctly and the **No** card if it is incorrectly identified.

Oral Language Activity 2

MATERIALS

Large noun cards (from Lessons A & B)

Large adjective cards

Over/Under cards

Yes/No cards

ID cards and instructor-made age cards with ages over and under 18

Pictures of men and women, teenagers, and children of various ages

OK/Not OK cards

Introduce the Target Verbs, Adjectives, and Prepositions

1. Say each target verb, adjective, or preposition for the group, pronouncing each term slowly and clearly.

> **I:** "Check." (Show the learners how to check an ID for age. Motion for the group to repeat together.)
>
> **G:** "Check."
>
> **I:** "Good. Check." (Model checking an ID for age. Motion for the group to repeat.)
>
> **G:** "Check."
>
> **I:** "Check." (Motion for the group to repeat.)
>
> **G:** "Check."

2. Expand to present the verb phrase **check ID.** Follow the format above.

3. Introduce the other target vocabulary (**give consent, illegal, legal, over,** and **under**) using the method above and the suggested cards and realia (see below) to clarify the meaning. For adjectives and prepositions, prompt with the **legal/illegal** and **over/under** cards.

Suggestions for Teaching Verbs, Adjectives, and Prepositions

Give consent—Explain **giving consent** using the **Yes** card. Associate **giving consent** with being 18 or older

Illegal—Show the **illegal** and **Not OK** cards to explain the meaning. If necessary, show pictures of someone doing an illegal act, e.g., stealing. Use the **sex** card from Lesson A and the **minor** card to associate sex with a minor as illegal and Not OK

Legal—Show the **legal** and **OK** cards to explain the meaning. Use the **sex** card from Lesson A and the **adult** card to associate sex with an adult as legal and OK

Over, Under—Hold a piece of paper or a book above and below a table or desk to convey the physical meaning of **over** and **under.** Put the list of ages from Oral Language Activity 1 on the board or on chart paper. Pick an age on the list and identify the other ages as over or under the chosen age. Repeat with a different age on the list to reinforce the terms. Use **adult** as an example of anyone age 18 and over, and use **minor** as an example of anyone under the age of 18

4. Say each word and have the group repeat each one three times.

5. Repeat any words more than three times as necessary (with the group, with pairs, or individually).

Concept Development and Sorting Activity

1. Make two columns, one for **18 and over/legal** and the other for **under 18/illegal,** on the board or on chart paper. Put the **adult** and **legal** cards at the top of one column and the **minor** and **illegal** cards at the top of the other column.

2. Use pictures of men, women, and teenagers and the ID and age cards to demonstrate for learners how to sort the pictures and the IDs into the two categories.

> **I:** "Man. Woman." (Hold up a picture of a man and a picture of a woman. Point to each picture while identifying it.)
>
> **I:** "Adult or minor?" (Put an ID card next to each picture. Use cards of the appropriate gender, with ages above 18 (such as the ages noted below). Point to the ID cards next to each picture.)
>
> **I:** "Check ID." (Look at the ID cards. Point to the ages on the IDs. Motion for the group to repeat.)
>
> **G:** "Check ID."
>
> **I:** "Woman is 25. Man is 26. OK?" (Motion for the group to respond.)
>
> **G:** "OK."
>
> **I:** "OK to give consent?" (Point to the woman. Point to the man. Motion for a response.)
>
> **G:** "Yes."

3. Put the pictures and the associated ID or age cards in the column for **over 18/legal.**

4. Introduce another "couple" using a pair of pictures in which one individual is not an adult. Alternate between the man or woman being the minor.

5. Using the method above, have learners determine that it is not OK to give consent if one person in a couple is a minor. Have the learners place the pictures and the ID cards in the correct column.

6. Present another example in which both people are minors. Follow the method above and place the pictures and IDs in the correct column.

7. Practice with other "couples," some above 18 and legal, some with one or both parties under 18.

8. Assist the group as necessary to make sure they can readily assign couples to the **legal** or **illegal** columns.

Comprehension Check

1. Collect the ID and age cards used in the sorting activity and shuffle them.

2. Introduce the cards one by one, identifying the person as a minor or an adult correctly and incorrectly at random.

3. Have learners say Yes when the card is correctly identified and No when it is incorrectly identified.

> **I:** "Minor?" (Hold up an ID or age card of a 16-year-old. Motion for a response.)
>
> **G:** "Yes." (Hold up the **Yes** card.)
>
> **I:** "Adult?" (Hold up an ID or age card of a 17-year-old. Motion for a response.)
>
> **G:** "No."

Oral Language Activity 3

Introduce the Target Sentences

MATERIALS

Large vocabulary cards

Instructor-made age cards

Pictures of men and women

Yes/No cards

1. Model the target sentences for the group while holding up corresponding cards to convey the meaning.

> **I:** "Sex with a minor is illegal." (Hold up the **sex, minor,** and **illegal** cards. Motion for the group to repeat together.)
>
> **G:** "Sex with a minor is illegal."
>
> **I:** "Sex with a minor is illegal." (Hold up the **sex, minor,** and **illegal** cards. Motion for the group to repeat together.)
>
> **G:** "Sex with a minor is illegal."
>
> **I:** "Sex with a minor is illegal." (Motion for the group to repeat. Put the cards at the front of the room.)
>
> **G:** "Sex with a minor is illegal."

2. If learners have difficulty repeating the entire sentence, break it into parts. Use backward buildup to present the parts and help learners master the sentence as a whole.
3. Model the second target sentence, using corresponding cards. Follow the method above. Use backward buildup to help learners repeat the entire sentence if necessary, as indicated on the following page.

> **I:** "It is illegal for a minor to say Yes."
>
> **I:** ". . . to say Yes." (Hold up the **Yes** card. Motion for the group to repeat.)
>
> **G:** ". . . to say Yes."
>
> **I:** ". . . for a minor . . ." (Hold up the **minor** card. Motion for the group to repeat.)
>
> **G:** ". . . for a minor . . ."
>
> **I:** ". . . for a minor to say Yes." (Hold up the **minor** and **Yes** cards. Motion for the group to repeat.)
>
> **G:** ". . . for a minor to say Yes."
>
> **I:** "It is illegal . . ." (Hold up the **illegal** card. Motion for a response.)
>
> **G:** "It is illegal . . ."
>
> **I:** "It is illegal for a minor to say Yes." (Point to the **illegal, minor,** and **Yes** cards. Motion for the group to repeat.)
>
> **G:** "It is illegal for a minor to say Yes."

4. Say each sentence and have the group repeat each one three times.
5. Repeat each sentence more than three times as necessary (with the group, with pairs, or individually).
6. Give additional practice with any words or phrases within the sentences that learners have difficulty with.

Age of Consent Activity

1. Shuffle instructor-made age cards with the ID cards.
2. Place the cards facedown in a pile in the center of the group.
3. Have each learner take a turn picking a card and identifying the age on the card or the age of the person on the ID, as in the example below.
4. Ask learners to state whether the age is legal or illegal for sexual relationships.
5. Model the activity for learners.

> **I:** "What's this?" (Pick a card from the pile, turn it over, and say the age on the card.)
>
> **I:** "Sixteen." (Hold up a card for **16** (ID or age) and show it to learners. Motion for learners to repeat.)
>
> **L:** "Sixteen."
>
> **I:** "Legal or illegal?" (Hold up the **16** and **sex** cards. Motion for a response.)
>
> **L:** "Illegal."
>
> **I:** "Sex with a minor is illegal." (Point to the **16** and **sex** cards. Motion for the group to repeat.)
>
> **G:** "Sex with a minor is illegal."

6. After a learner picks an ID or age card and states the age, hold up the **sex** card and ask if sex with a person that age is legal or illegal. If it is illegal, have learners repeat the target sentence **Sex with a minor is illegal.**

7. Adapt the method above to have the group practice the target sentence **It is illegal for a minor to say Yes.**

8. After a learner picks a card and states the age, hold up the **sex** card and ask if sex with a person that age is legal or illegal. Associate the age card with saying Yes, to give consent for sex. Ask if that consent is legal or illegal. If it is illegal, have learners repeat the target sentence **It is illegal for a minor to say Yes.**

> **I:** "What's this?" (Hold up an age or ID card for **17** and motion for a response.)
>
> **L:** "Seventeen."
>
> **I:** "Legal or illegal?" (Hold up the **17** and **sex** cards. Motion for a response.)
>
> **L:** "Illegal."
>
> **I:** "Seventeen says Yes." (Hold up the **17**, **sex**, and **Yes** cards to associate a 17-year-old with saying Yes to a sexual relationship.)
>
> **I:** Legal or illegal? (Hold up the **17**, **sex**, and **Yes** cards. Motion for a response.)
>
> **G:** Illegal.
>
> **I:** "It is illegal for a minor to say Yes." (Point to the **picture, age,** and **Yes** cards. Motion for the group to repeat.)
>
> **G:** "It is illegal for a minor say Yes."

9. Continue practice with other ages, over and under 18, to give practice with the concept and the target sentences.

Comprehension Check

1. Distribute **Yes/No** cards to each learner.
2. Hold up different age cards and ask learners if the age to give consent is legal or illegal.

> **I:** "Sixteen. Legal?" (Hold up the **16** and **legal** cards. Motion for a response.)
>
> **G:** "No."
>
> **I:** "Twenty-four. Legal? (Hold up the **24** and **legal** cards. Motion for a response.)
>
> **G:** "Yes"

3. Have the learners hold up the **Yes** card if the match is legal and the **No** card if it is illegal.

4. Continue with a variety of ages to ensure learners' understanding of which ones are legal and which are not.
5. Assist learners as necessary.

Oral Language Activity 4

Introduce the Dialogue

1. Write the sample dialogue (see example below) on the board or other visible surface.
2. Model the dialogue by pointing to each line as it is said, using corresponding cards and realia.

> **Speaker 1:** "What should you do?" (Hold up an ID card. Motion for a response.)
> **Speaker 2:** "Check age."
> **Speaker 1:** "What is legal?" (Hold up the **adult** card. Motion for a response.)
> **Speaker 2:** "Eighteen and over—legal to say Yes."
> **Speaker 1:** "What is illegal?" (Hold up the **minor** card. Motion for a response.)
> **Speaker 2:** "Under 18—illegal to say Yes."

3. Introduce the dialogue with the instructor as Speaker 1 and the learners as Speaker 2. If necessary, model the learners' response and have them repeat.
4. Make sure that learners can respond to each verbal and visual prompt before continuing on to the dialogue activity.

Dialogue Activity

1. Review the question/answer pairs from the dialogue. Ask the question and prompt learners visually using cards and realia as appropriate for the desired response.
2. If necessary, assist learners by modeling the response and having them repeat.

> **I:** "What should you do?" (Hold up an ID card. Motion for a response.)
> **G:** "Check age."

3. Continue with the activity by prompting learners visually and verbally using cards and realia as appropriate for the desired response.

> **I:** "What should you do?" (Hold up an ID card. Motion for a response.)
>
> **G:** "Check age."
>
> **I:** "What is legal?" (Hold up the **adult** card. Motion for a response.)
>
> **G:** "Eighteen and over—legal to say Yes."
>
> **I:** "What is illegal?" (Hold up the **minor** card. Motion for a response.)
>
> **G:** "Under 18—illegal to say Yes."

4. Repeat the couplets by holding up cards in random order to prompt learners' responses.
5. Assist the group as necessary.

Comprehension Check

1. Spread the instructor-made age cards and the ID cards faceup on a table or other visible surface.
2. Say the terms **legal** or **illegal** to the group.
3. Ask learners to listen and point to or pick up age cards that are legal or illegal for giving consent to sexual relationships.
4. Have learners repeat the term that is said each time.

> **I:** "Legal." (Motion for the group to find ages 18 or above.)
>
> **G:** "Legal." (Learners should point to or pick up ages of 18 or above.)
>
> **I:** "Illegal." (Motion for the group to find ages 17 and under.)
>
> **G:** "Illegal." (Learners should point to or pick up ages of 17 or under.)

5. Repeat and vary calling for legal and illegal choices at random to ensure the group's comprehension of the concept.

Reading Activity

MATERIALS

Large vocabulary cards

Circle the Correct Word activity sheet (one enlarged and one per learner)

Review

1. Shuffle all of the target vocabulary cards.
2. Show each card to the group while pronouncing each word slowly and clearly.
3. Run a finger under each word to help learners begin to recognize the words apart from the pictures.
4. Have the learners repeat the words at least three times.

> **I:** "Age." (Point to the word.)
> **G:** "Age."
> **I:** "Age." (Underline the word with a finger. Motion for the group to repeat the word.)
> **G:** "Age."

5. Continue to review with the cards, using the pattern above.
6. Fold cards in half to show only the words, to help learners become less dependent on the pictures.
7. Move from group to individual practice as learners become more comfortable reading the words without the assistance of the pictures.

Circle the Correct Word Activity

1. Display the large vocabulary cards from Lesson B in a visible location for learners' reference.
2. Distribute a Circle the Correct Word activity sheet to each learner.
3. Post an enlarged activity sheet in the front of the room or other visible location.
4. Using the enlarged activity sheet, ask learners to look at and identify each picture.
5. Use one item as an example to show learners how to complete the activity sheet.
6. Help learners to use the large vocabulary cards to match the picture in the example to one of the words listed next to the picture.
7. On the enlarged activity sheet, demonstrate how to find the word that corresponds to the picture.
8. Show learners on that example item how to circle the word that corresponds to the picture.

> **I:** "Adult." (Motion for learners to look at the list of words.)
> **I:** "Here it is. Adult." (Model circling the corresponding word. Have learners circle the word on their own activity sheet.)

9. Complete the activity sheet as a group.

Writing Activity

Review

1. Shuffle all of the target vocabulary cards.
2. Show each card to the group while pronouncing each word slowly and clearly.

3. Run a finger under each word to help learners begin to recognize the words apart from the pictures.
4. Have the learners repeat the words at least three times.

> **I:** "Adult." (Point to the word.)
> **G:** "Adult."
> **I:** "Adult." (Underline the word with a finger. Motion for the group to repeat the word.)
> **G:** "Adult."

NOTE

Separating words from pictures should be done gradually and after plenty of practice.

5. Continue to review with the cards, using the pattern above.
6. Fold cards in half to show only the words, to help learners become less dependent on the pictures.
7. Move from group to individual practice as learners become more comfortable reading the words without the assistance of the pictures.

Write the Dialogue Activity

1. Distribute a Write the Dialogue activity sheet to each learner.
2. Place an enlarged version of the activity sheet in the front of the room or in another visible location.
3. Display the large vocabulary cards from Lesson B in a visible location for learners' reference.
4. Take the role of Speaker 1 and say the question in each couplet from the dialogue. On the enlarged copy of the activity sheet, point to each word as you say it.
5. Ask the group to read along with the dialogue responses and fill in the missing words in the dialogue as they say the response. Use the pictures to prompt learners with the missing words.
6. On the enlarged activity sheet, model how to write the missing words on the lines in the responses.
7. Have learners write the words on their own activity sheets.
8. Read through the dialogue as Speaker 1 and have the group respond as Speaker 2, using their completed activity sheets.
9. Assist learners as necessary.

NOTE

If any learner finds this difficult, write the word or phrase on the activity sheet above the appropriate picture and have the learner trace what is written.

4 Unit Review Activity

MATERIALS

Unit Review activity sheet (one enlarged and one per learner)

Large vocabulary cards (from Lessons A & B)

NOTE

The Unit Review Activity can be done as a group activity for reinforcing the concepts learned in the lesson or done as an individual activity for assessment purposes.

OK or Not OK Review Activity

1. Use large vocabulary cards from Lessons A and B to review the vocabulary and concepts of the unit.
2. Post an enlarged copy of the activity sheet in the front of the room or in another visible location.
3. Point to each picture on the enlarged activity sheet and ask learners to identify it. Make sure learners understand the symbol for No (circle with slash) to indicate that what is pictured is not done or used.
4. Distribute a copy of the Unit Review activity sheet to each learner.
5. On the enlarged activity sheet, point to the pair of pictures in each item. Elicit from learners whether the action or choice and result in the item is OK (desirable or legal) or Not OK (not desirable or illegal).
6. Ask learners to complete the activity on their own sheets. If necessary, use the enlarged activity sheet to model for learners how to check the correct column to indicate that the item is OK or Not OK.

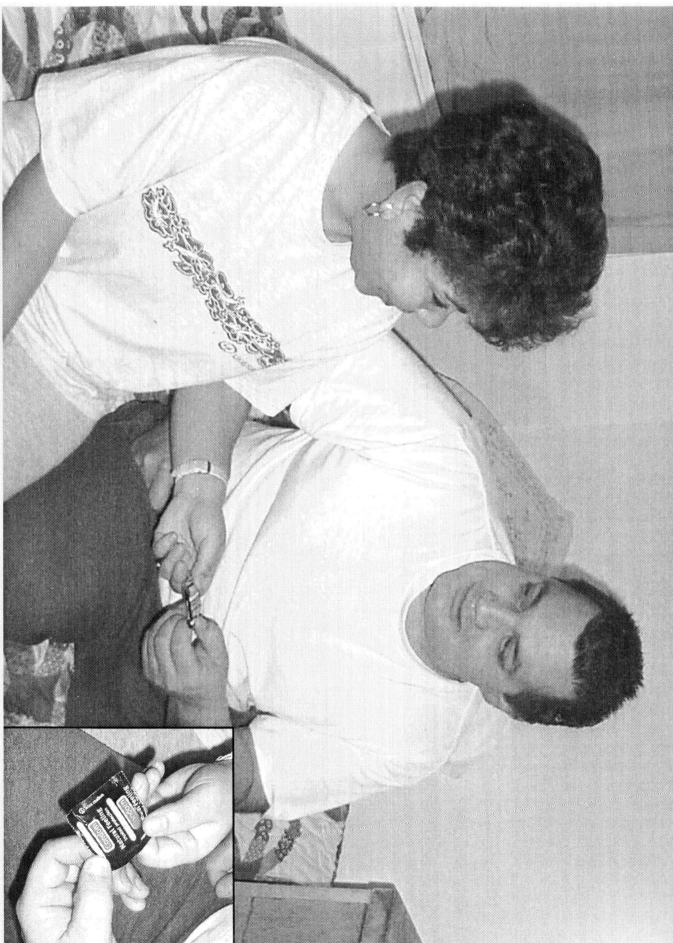

Central Theme Picture

Latex condom

Disease

Man

Pregnancy

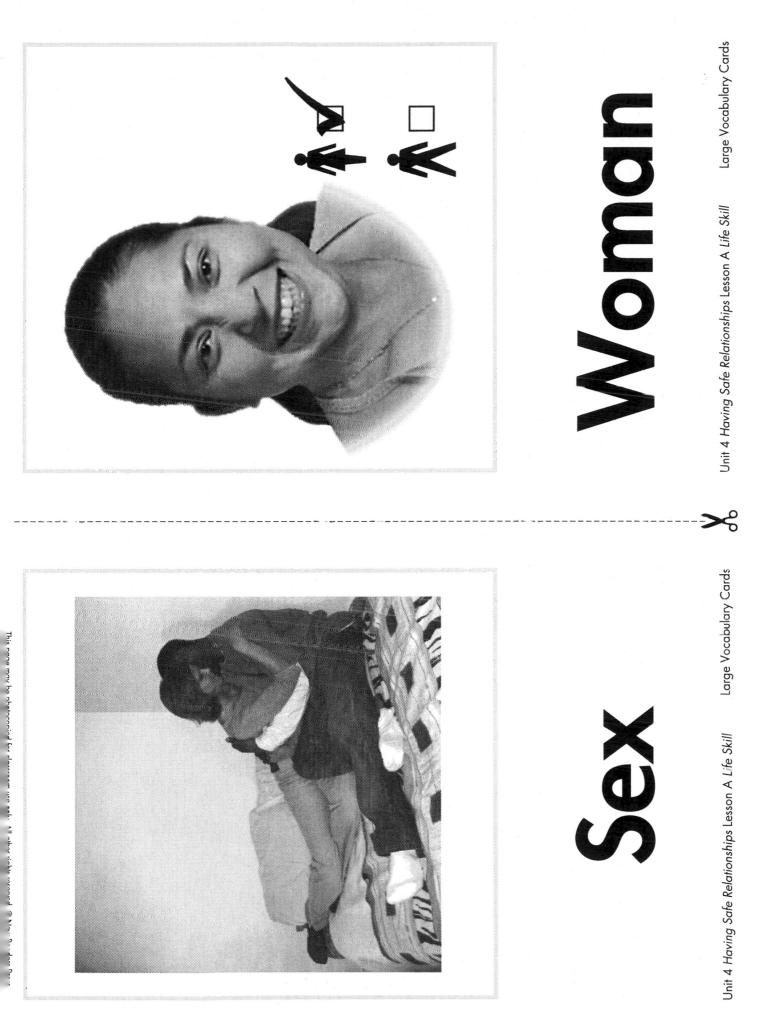

Woman

Unit 4 *Having Safe Relationships* Lesson A *Life Skill*

Sex

Unit 4 *Having Safe Relationships* Lesson A *Life Skill*

No

Yes

Mini Picture Bingo   Board 1

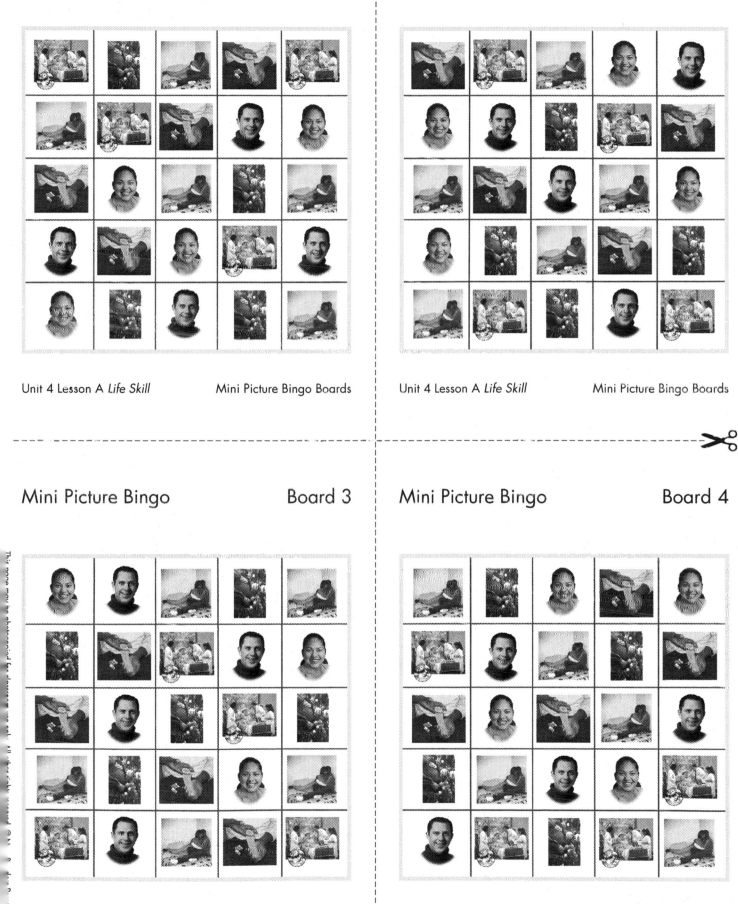

Mini Picture Bingo   Board 2

Mini Picture Bingo   Board 3

Mini Picture Bingo   Board 4

Graphic Organizer Activity

Look at the graphic organizer. Read it as a group.

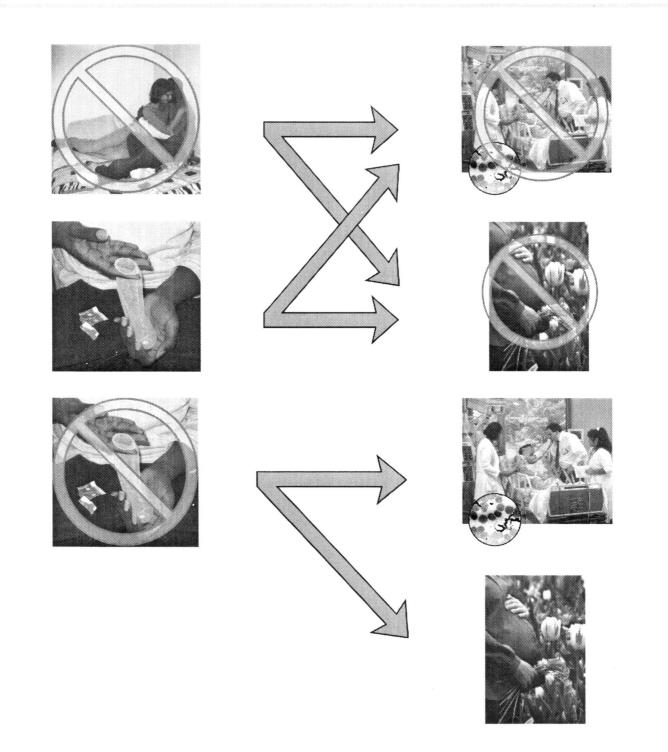

Write the Dialogue Activity

Look at the pictures. Fill in the missing words. Complete the dialogue.

1. **Speaker 1:** What do you choose?

   Speaker 2: _____ _____.

No

2. **Speaker 1:** What do you choose?

   Speaker 2: _____ _____.

No

3. **Speaker 1:** What do you choose?

   Speaker 2: _____ _____.

No

4. **Speaker 1:** What do you choose?

   Speaker 2: _____ _____.

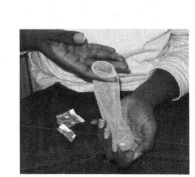

Adult

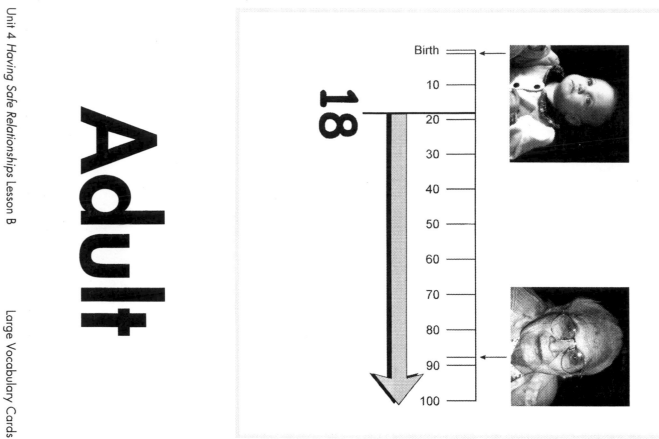

18

Birth
10
20
30
40
50
60
70
80
90
100

Age

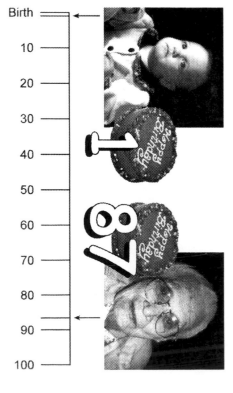

Birth
10
20
30
40
50
60
70
80
90
100

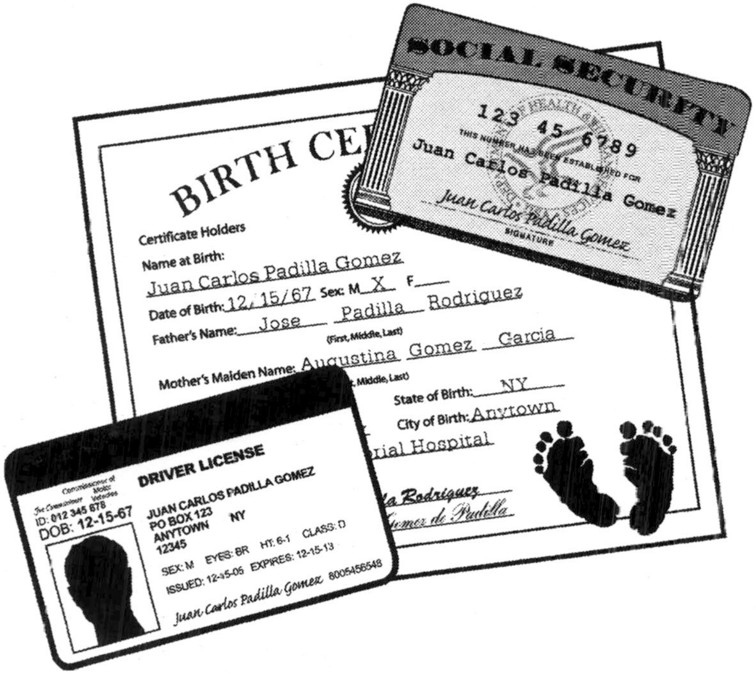

ID

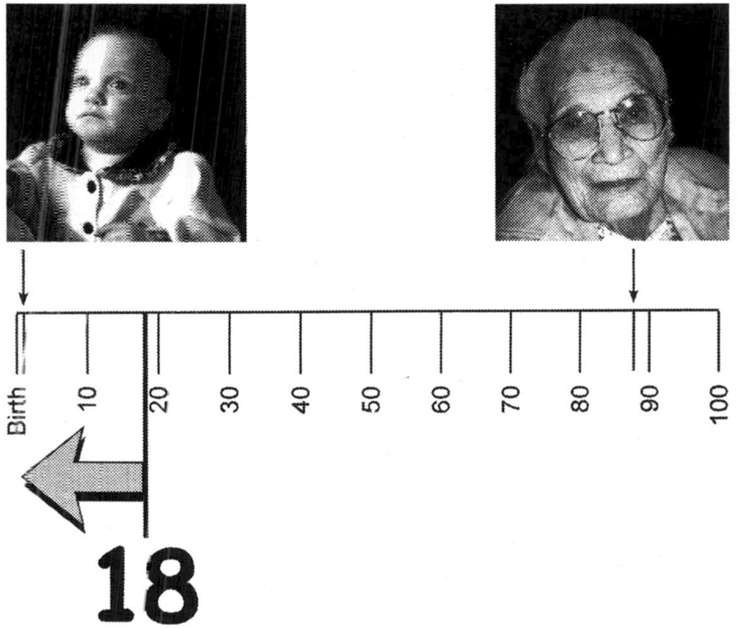

Minor

Unit 4 *Having Safe Relationships* Lesson B Large Vocabulary Cards

Illegal

Legal

Over

Large Vocabulary Cards

Unit 4 *Having Safe Relationships* Lesson B

Under

Large Vocabulary Cards

Unit 4 *Having Safe Relationships* Lesson B

Picture ID

Name: Christine Kim

DOB: 07 / 21 / 90

Picture ID

Name: Ahmed Hassan

DOB: 02 / 09 / 87

Picture ID

Name: Grace Lin

DOB: 03 / 27 / 89

Picture ID

Name: Pavel Gagarin

DOB: 08 / 20 / 71

Picture ID

Name: Thomas Majok

DOB: 10 / 05 / 79

Picture ID

Name: Carlos Fuentes

DOB: 04 / 30 / 90

Picture ID

Name: Carmen Reyna

DOB: 11 / 06 / 85

STATE DRIVER'S LICENSE

Commissioner of Motor Vehicles
Joe Commissioner
ID: 012 345 678
DOB: 12-15-80

DRIVER LICENSE

MARCO HERNANDEZ
PO BOX 123
ANYTOWN   NY
12345

SEX: M   EYES: BR   HT: 6-1   CLASS: D

ISSUED: 12-15-05 EXPIRES: 12-15-13

Marco Hernandez   8005456548

Unit 4 *Having Safe Relationships* Lesson B *Civic Responsibility*

ID Cards

Circle the Correct Word Activity

Look at each picture. Circle the correct word.

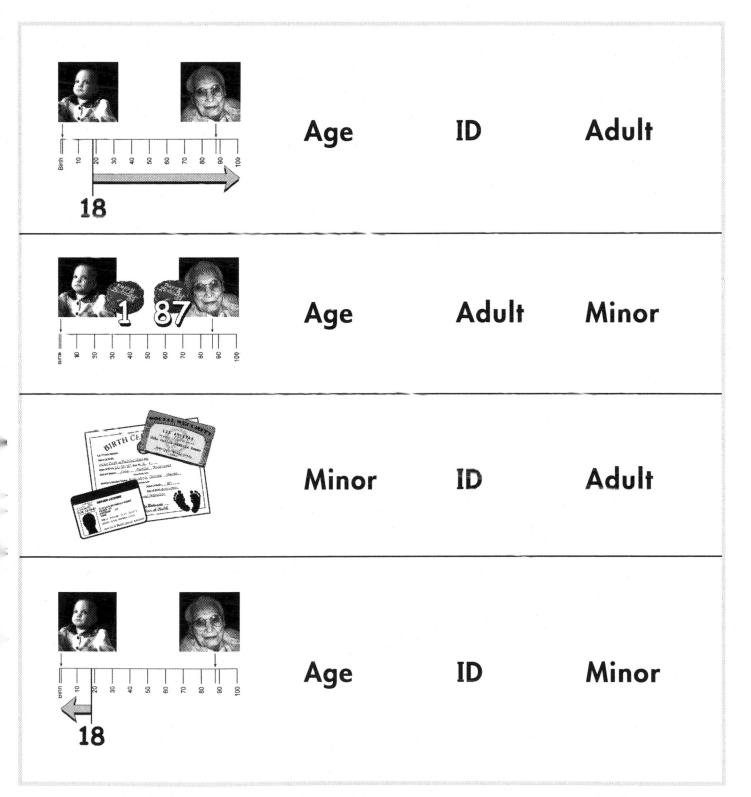

Age	ID	Adult
Age	Adult	Minor
Minor	ID	Adult
Age	ID	Minor

Unit 4 *Having Safe Relationships* Lesson B *Civic Responsibility*

Reading Activity Sheet

Write the Dialogue Activity

Use the pictures. Write the missing words. Complete the dialogue.

Speaker 1: What should you do?

Speaker 2: Check _____ _____ .

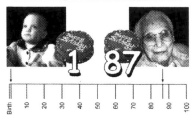

Speaker 1: What is legal?

Speaker 2: _____ and over—legal for an _____ to say Yes.

Speaker 1: What is illegal?

Speaker 2: Under _____—illegal for a _____ to say Yes.

Directions: Look at the sets of pictures. Check OK or Not OK.

	OK	Not OK
	_____	_____
	_____	_____
	_____	_____
18	_____	_____
18	_____	_____
	_____	_____

OK

Not OK